THERE'S NO BUSINESS LIKE SHOW BUSINESS

(but I wouldn't ditch my day job)

THERE'S NO BUSINESS LIKE SHOW BUSINESS

(but I wouldn't ditch my day job)

HONEST ED MIRVISH

KEY PORTER BOOKS

Canadian Cataloguing in Publication Data

Mirvish, Ed, 1914–

    There's no business like show business : but I wouldn't
    ditch my day job

Includes index.
ISBN 1-55013-875-8

1. Mirvish, Ed, 1914–　. 2. Royal Alexandra Theatre (Toronto, Ont.) –
Anecdotes. 3. Theater – Ontario – Toronto – Anecdotes. I. Title.

PN2308.M57A3　　　1997　　　　　792'.092　　　　　C97-932041-0

The publisher gratefully acknowledges the
support of the Canada Council for the Arts
and the Ontario Arts Council for its
publishing program.

THE CANADA COUNCIL | LE CONSEIL DES ARTS
FOR THE ARTS | DU CANADA
SINCE 1957 | DEPUIS 1957

Key Porter Books Limited
70 The Esplanade
Toronto, Ontario
Canada M5E 1R2

Printed and bound in Canada

97 98 99 00　6 5 4 3 2 1

*This book is dedicated
to our audiences, because without you
there'd be no book.*

Acknowledgements

To the following six people, my sincere gratitude:

Russell Lazar, Honest Ed's diligent general manager, for all his research and excellent suggestions.

Robert Brockhouse, Mirvish Productions' suave literary manager, for reminding me of additional stories.

Anne Mirvish, my talented wife—who deserves total credit for introducing me to theatre's roar of the crowd in the first place—for her constant support through the years.

David Mirvish, our bright if unpretentious son who, within recent years, has brought such shows as *Les Miz, Miss Saigon, Crazy for You, Jane Eyre*, and *Rent* to Toronto. I am proud of all his accomplishments.

Anna Porter, my publisher, for spurring me to create a second book of my memoirs by once more offering me money.

Paul King, my friend, who again gave his invaluable advice and professional help in penning and polishing this book, as he did with the first.

Foreword

Ed Mirvish is timeless.

He has presented some of the greatest artists in the world—and is as great an artist as any of them, since the man created a theatrical renaissance.

When I first played Toronto in the 1950s, it was a pretty stiff town. Then Ed and his family came along and influenced a change that today places Toronto on a par with any other great world city. They did amazing things in Toronto. And then in England.

Wherever I have travelled I've never met a fan who does not relish Toronto's live theatre, and Ed Mirvish, an amazing and creative artist, is singularly responsible for that.

I wish he was a citizen of the United States—to help keep our own arts flourishing.

I love him.

Tony Bennett

Preface

On April 1, 1930, my father, David Mirvish, lay in a back-room bed behind our grocery store on downtown Toronto's Dundas Street. At two in the morning, at the age of 42, he died.

My mother, completely exhausted, had fallen asleep with my younger brother and sister. I was holding my father's hand.

With my father gone, I had to drop out of my third year in high school and at the age of 15 became a storekeeper.

Today at eighty-three, I am still a storekeeper—going to Honest Ed's, our huge world-famous bargain emporium on Bloor Street every morning at eight, and dining in one of our King Street restaurants each noon.

Yet, for the past 35 years, my family's also been in the theatre business. I bought two historic theatres in Toronto and London, England, the Royal Alex and the Old Vic, and then our son, David, built the newest in North America, the Princess of Wales.

But as much as I've grown to love the theatre business, I've never given up my day job at Honest Ed's and the restaurants. In fact, I never will. And I'll tell you why.

Through the years I've discovered that bargains are

dependable and predictable. I can say the same about roast beef dinners.

I can't say the same about the theatre. It is—as some of the following stories will show—totally unpredictable, extremely high risk, and frequently a major aggravation.

What makes it so overwhelmingly attractive is this. When it works, it is more rewarding than any vocation you could possibly be involved in.

When you see entire audiences stand with thunderous ovations and hear those waves of applause roll over the footlights, there's no other experience like it in the world.

When a show wins raves, I must admit, it also adds considerably more prestige than I'm used to as a storekeeper.

And finally, a hugely successful theatrical hit can support you financially the rest of your life. And I certainly enjoy that aspect of it.

But regardless of the excitement, the kudos, and the cash, I'm still at heart a storekeeper. And not a bad one.

Which is why, although I love showbiz, I'd never ditch my day job.

THERE'S NO BUSINESS LIKE SHOW BUSINESS

(but I wouldn't ditch my day job)

I should really dedicate this book to Cawthra Mulock. If it weren't for Cawthra, I'd never have been in the theatre business. Because if he hadn't *built* the Royal Alexandra, I couldn't have *bought* it.

What's more, he saved me a lot of money. It cost *$535,000 less* to buy the theatre than he paid to put it up half a century before.

Though the man's been dead now for nearly 80 years, I like him a lot.

In 1906, at the age of 21, Cawthra Mulock was Canada's youngest millionaire. He was scion of two rich old Toronto families, the Cawthras (who'd made a fortune importing apothecary goods) and the Mulocks (who'd made their wealth from an iron works). And when Sir William Mulock, a Supreme Court of Ontario Justice, married a Cawthra, they bestowed their joint names, and wealth, on their son.

And the son was no slouch. He bought a seat on the stock exchange and swiftly doubled his inheritance. Sailing often to Europe's capitals on business, young Mulock fell madly in love with the theatre. Back in Toronto, the theatre he loved most was the Princess on King Street, which specialized in musicals.

One evening, however, after standing in line for tickets, he arrived at the wicket to find the show sold out. It made Mulock mad. Here he was, worth millions, and couldn't buy a seat. So he decided to build his own theatre. On May 8, 1906, Mulock bought a lot near the theatre district, on King just west of Simcoe.

It was land originally owned by Sir John Colborne, one of the "Iron Duke's" soldiers at the Battle of Waterloo and latterly Ontario's lieutenant-governor. He'd bequeathed the property to Upper Canada College. Although the college had since moved to the sticks above St. Clair, a few school buildings still remained on the site when Mulock bought it.

On King and Simcoe's southeast corner stood the stately stone Church of St. Andrew, and beside it the regal Government House, residence of the lieutenant-governor. Across the street sat the bustling British Tavern, vastly popular with the area's theatrical actors, but despised by St. Andrew's staunch Presbyterians.

Because of these structures, the four corners were called Education, Salvation, Legislation, and Damnation. Today, sadly or gladly, depending on one's viewpoint, only Salvation remains.

To erect his new theatre, Mulock hired 34-year-old architect John Lyle, a recent graduate of the Ecole des beaux-arts in Paris who later designed two other great Toronto landmarks: Union Station, and the Bank of Nova Scotia's building at Bay and King.

Steeped in the "French Renaissance" style that he

brought to his theatre design, Lyle's only instruction from Mulock was to "build me the finest theatre on the continent."

Lyle took Cawthra seriously. Tossing away his budget, he created one of the world's finest theatres—an Edwardian jewel box of fine imported marble, tiles and velvets, hand-carved walnut and cherrywood, crystal chandeliers, silken wall coverings and gilded plaster—while importing European craftsmen to shape them.

John Lyle's designs were revolutionary. With the thickest walls of any North American theatre, this was the first on the continent to feature balconies without internal pillars to interrupt sightlines, the first to be fireproofed, and the first in the world to be air-conditioned.

While Lyle and his artisans toiled, Mulock went to London and, using his family connections, got a patent from King Edward VII to name his consort, Princess Alexandra of Denmark, as the theatre's patron—as well as receiving the official right to call the theatre "Royal."

By the time he got home, the theatre was complete. Its total cost was $750,000—a staggering sum at a time when a really good wage was 25 cents an hour. Mulock, however, could not only afford it, but was thrilled at the result.

Weeks later, on August 26, 1907, the Royal Alex

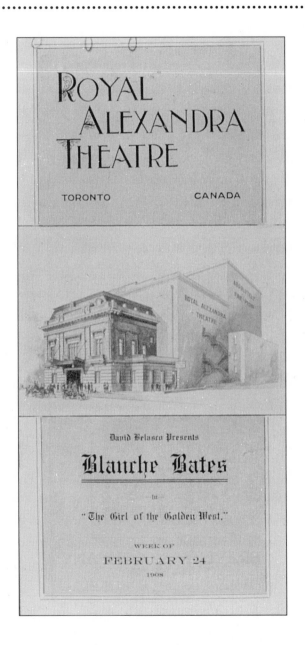

opened its doors to the world—with the Schubert Company's musical extravaganza *Top o' the World*, featuring a cast of more than 100. It set the tone for the Royal Alexandra to showcase the biggest shows and greatest of stars.

And they soon appeared in its spotlights—such luminaries as De Wolfe Hopper, Eddie Foy, George M. Cohan, Ed Wynn, Marie Dressler, and Lillian Gish.

But the Alex didn't just stick to slick big-star Broadway fare. It hosted the greatest classical actors and tragedians of the day such as Edward H. Robins, Sir Johnston Forbes-Robertson, Otis Skinner, Edith Evans, Robert Bruce Mantell, and Katharine Cornell.

It also encouraged new Canadian theatre by providing a home stage for the famous Dora Mavor Moore and Vaughan Glaser troupes, as well as giving a home base to The Dumbells, that zany comedy troupe of Canadian soldiers who became renowned during World War I and later toured with revues across the country.

Yet during the post-war years, the neighbourhood began to fade in ways Mulock (who in 1918, aged 33, died of Spanish flu) could not have foreseen. When the Alex was built, it occupied a beautiful park-like setting.

One of the earliest playbills from the Royal Alex—
February 1908.

*King Street and the Royal Alex: a far cry from the busy
street we know today.*

King Street was a broad, tree-shaded boulevard, lined by
grand structures. Ladies out for a day of shopping would
stop for lunch in the theatre's second-floor French
Lounge, open daily as an elegant tea room.

The deterioration began when the massive
Parliament Buildings that abutted Simcoe Street were
demolished, and the Grand Trunk Railway began building warehouses on the site. Soon after, the magnificent
Government House was razed, this time by the Canadian
Pacific Railway, and an office building was erected on the
land.

Before long, the south side of King Street was filled with tracks and marshalling yards, the north side crammed with warehouses and freight sheds, and the air was pungent with soot and smoke. Ironically, the proximity of the railroad tracks proved a partial advantage to the Alex, since it made the transport of sets and props far easier. But the district was in steep decline.

The years after World War II saw a gradual drying up of touring companies across the continent, although the Alex kept drawing such names as Maurice Evans, Edith Piaf, Paul Muni, Raymond Massey, Julie Harris, José Ferrer, and Charlton Heston, who made his professional debut in *Antony and Cleopatra* on its stage.

By the late fifties, however, the grey industrial area had become derelict and desolate. All the other great old theatres (the Princess, the Grand Opera House, Shea's Hippodrome) had been torn down or converted into movie houses (the Elgin, the Pantages, the Uptown). Finally, by the early sixties, the Royal Alex itself was up for sale.

This was the historic theatre that actors, architects, and the public all loved. Stripper Gypsy Rose Lee (who played it in the *Threepenny Opera*) said of the Alex that it was "the most beautiful, delightful theatre I know. It would break my heart if anything happened to it." And singer Al Jolson (the man whose father, a rabbi, had circumcised me) proclaimed it as "the only theatre that makes my voice sound better than I think it does."

But the Cawthra Mulock Trust, which owned it, needed money. None of the other theatre companies could afford it. The City of Toronto, which already owned the O'Keefe Centre, wasn't interested. Toronto Hydro, who *did* want to buy it, was refused because they wanted to raze it for a parking lot.

And that, folks, is where I came in.

My wife, Anne, and son, David, had always loved theatre. I had always loved a bargain. The Alex looked like something we could go together with. So we made a bid. And in 1962, we bought the Royal Alex for $215,000 cash.

The only stipulation was our promise not to raze it but to run it as a legitimate theatre for at least five years. After that, we could do with the building whatever we wanted.

I made a lot of sceptics chuckle when I promised, "It will always be a theatre, even if I have to run it at a loss." To prove it, we immediately spent nearly double the purchase cost to restore it. We hired interior decorator

We tried to maintain the wonderful ornate architectural details, such as this one from the first balcony, to keep the glorious opulence alive.

Herbert Irvine, and architects Allward and Guinlock, and paraphrasing Cawthra Mulock's original request, I told them, "I want the Royal Alex once again to be the finest theatre on the continent."

In only seven months, with teams of craftsmen working on scaffolds, they brilliantly revitalized the Old Lady of King Street into her former turn-of-the-century splendour. The only main changes were converting the former tea room into an elegant bar, erecting a new marquee with 1,363 flashing lights out front, and installing new air-conditioning.

The gala reopening was on Monday, September 9, 1963, with a comedy called *Never Too Late*, which I'll mention later. After a pre-show dinner for 70 guests at Winston's Grill, we were greeted at the theatre by stabbing searchlights and a media swarm. Celebrities in the audience included everyone from Lady Eaton to comics Wayne and Shuster, and at intermission actress June Havoc went on stage to say, "This is one of the loveliest theatres in the world. Love it back."

And thus was my baptism into showbiz.

As proprietor of Honest Ed's, I'd received scads of press coverage for our outlandish dance marathons, dogsled races, and triplets contests. But the day after the opening, the North American media attention I got dwarfed any publicity I'd ever received as a storekeeper.

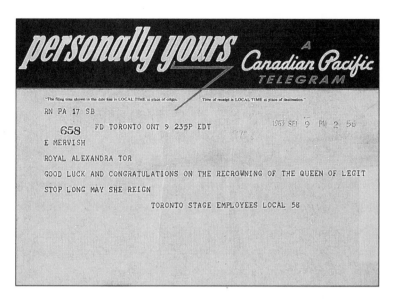

*Telegrams of congratulations are always welcome,
but this one from the union of stage employees was
especially nice to receive.*

The Globe and Mail reported, "Mr. Mirvish, in his
new and becoming role of patron of the arts, has lavished
taste, money and the talents of a brilliant decorator on
the Royal Alexandra."

Up till then, I wasn't a theatre-goer. I knew nothing
about theatre. And I wasn't qualified to run one. If I'd
known what I was getting into, I'd probably not have
touched the Alex. But I thought it was a bargain, so I
bought it.

And suddenly I was "a patron of the arts."

I'd also agreed to remain one for the next five years. Fortunately, at the end of that time, I'd formed a deep attachment to theatre and the people who keep it alive. Just as lucky was the fact that the Alex wasn't losing money and was sometimes in the black.

The first thing I'd learned was that as long as you kept a theatre locked, you knew exactly how much it cost each week. But as soon as you put a production on stage, you could go bankrupt very quickly. If you staged a show no one wanted to see, it was easy to drop a cool $50,000 a week.

One of the major things that saved us was building a huge subscription. With 52,000 subscribers on the list, every road show that played was 85 per cent sold out six weeks before it even arrived.

Somehow, through sheer ignorance, we've kept the Old Lady going through the decades. And in all that time, it's never been dark.

When we bought the Alex, the district was still dingy. I knew it would turn off audiences, unless we tried to clean it up. Since the CPR wouldn't part with its railroad tracks, we had to concentrate on the empty old buildings around us. Fortunately, we were able to buy two blocks of factories and warehouses to the immediate west. We painted them white, crammed them with antiques, and turned them into restaurants that are almost always packed.

King Street today is an absolute delight. There's not a track to be seen.

When I bought the Royal Alex, I at least knew what it looked like. When I bought the Old Vic, I'd never even laid eyes on the place. In fact, I'd never even been to London.

But on June 8, 1982, I got a call from a lawyer friend who told me the Old Vic was for sale. There was no set price, he told me; it was going to the highest bidder. But he'd heard that Andrew Lloyd Webber was bidding £500,000.

I said I'd think about it. "Well, you'd better think fast, Ed," he told me. "The bidding closes in 72 hours."

So David, Anne, and I sat down and talked it over. They both knew the theatre and loved it. So finally we decided to go for it.

But I still couldn't imagine that anyone, especially someone as shrewd as Lloyd Webber, the world's richest composer, would announce any price before a secret bid, unless he was bluffing.

So we bid £550,000. And, because I couldn't trust the mails, I flew a lawyer to London with the offer.

Two weeks later, we received a congratulatory cable from the trustees. The Mirvishes were the Old Vic's new owners.

It wasn't just the news that stunned me, but the fact that Lloyd Webber had *indeed* bid £500,000. I'd overbid him by about a hundred thousand bucks. So much for considering myself shrewd with a deal.

When I flew to London to deliver the cheque, I found that the British press was up in arms about a foreigner buying their historic landmark. So, at a massive press conference, I explained that I felt more like a temporary caretaker than an owner, since nobody really owned anything. And what's more, we intended to totally refurbish the Old Vic as we had the Royal Alex.

In closing, I said, "They're calling me a foreigner. But I'm really just a lad from the colonies." Thank God, they applauded. But scepticism lingered, until we actually began renovations—which were vital.

In 1982, the Old Vic was in exactly the same state as the Royal Alex was when I'd bought it 20 years before. Because of a £380,000 deficit, its trustees had put it up for sale.

This was a theatre that had seen the world's greatest

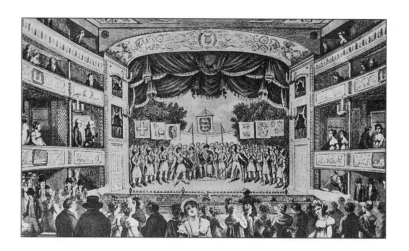

The Old Vic has a long and honoured history—I feel fortunate to be a part of that history. This is the opening night, May 11, 1818, of the Royal Coburg, which became the Old Vic.

actors on its stage since it opened 174 years before. During that time it had come to be called "the most famous theatre in the world." But the years had not been kind. The Old Vic had become a cultural relic of the Industrial Revolution. The only part of the original building remaining was its outer walls.

The theatre had been built in 1818 on soggy Lambeth Marsh of the Thames' south bank off Waterloo Road. Its owners had received royal patronage from Saxe-Coburg's Prince Leopold, but because it took two

ROYAL COBURG THEATRE.

(Opposite Waterloo-Bridge Road, Lambeth.)

Under the immediate Patronage of
HIS ROYAL HIGHNESS PRINCE LEOPOLD OF SAXE COBURG.

☞ The most flattering Applause has been conferred on the entirely New Entertainments produced at this New and Elegant Theatre; and the Proprietors respectfully assure their Patrons and numerous Friends, that no exertion shall be wanting on their part to render the Performances every way worthy of their continued support.

This present THURSDAY, May 13, & two following Evenings,
AN APPROPRIATE ADDRESS
(Written by JOSEPH LUNN, Esq.) will be spoken by Mr. MUNRO.

After which will be presented an entirely New Melo-Dramatic Spectacle, with New Music, Scenery, Dresses, &c. &c. called

TRIAL BY BATTLE;
OR, "HEAVEN DEFEND THE RIGHT!"

In which will be pourtrayed the ancient mode of decision by Kemp Fight, or Single Combat.

The Scenery painted by Messrs. MORRIS, SCRUTON, STANFIELD and WILKINS.
The Machinery by Messrs. LEWIS and CRADDOCK.   The Dresses by Mr. SMITHYES and Mr. CROSS.
The Properties Banners and Armour, by Mr. COLLET and Assistants.

THE MELO-DRAMA WRITTEN AND PRODUCED BY MR. W. BARRYMORE.

Baron Falconbridge .... Mr. MUNRO, from the Theatre-Royal, Edinburgh.
Albert ...... Mr. DAVIDGE, from the Sans Pareil.   Hilbert, *(his Son)* Mr. McCARTHY, from the Theatre-Royal, Bath.
Ambrose .... Mr. STEBBING, late of Astley's Royal Amphitheatre.   Barnard ...... Mr GALLOT, from the Theatre, Chester.
Rufus ...... Mr. BRADLEY, late of the Surrey Theatre.   Bath .... Mr. MORLEY, from the Surrey Theatre.
Henric .... Mr. T. BLANCHARD, from the Theatre, Liverpool.   Gilbert ...... Mr BRYANT, from the Surrey Theatre.
Little Jem .... Miss J. SCOTT, from the King's Theatre.
Morrice, *(a silly Peasant,)* .... Mr. HARWOOD, from the Theatre-Royal, York.
Chorus of Smugglers .... Messrs. Stanley, Clarke, Willis, Holman, Webster, Ducrow and George.
Geralda ...... Miss COOPER, from the Worthing Theatre.   Ninette .... Miss E. HOLLAND.
Ladies of the Court ...... Mesdames Nicals, Brag, Hart, Smith, Enscoe, and Baylis.
Knights, Squires, Herald, &c by the rest of the Company.

In the course of the Piece, a GLEE by Messrs. GALLOTT, MORLEY & NELSON.

After which, a Grand Asiatic Ballet, (composed and produced by Mr. Le Clercq, Ballet Master) with New Music, Scenery, Dresses and Decorations, called

ALZORA AND NERINE;
OR, THE FAIRY GIFT.

THE SCENERY PAINTED BY MR. SCRUTON.

Alzora *(an Eastern Prince,)* .... Mr. LE CLERCQ.
His Suite... Mr. Gay; Mr. Cartlitch; Masters Ashbury and Honner; Mesers. Stanley, Holman, Clarke, Willis, Webster, Simpson, George and Ducrow; Misses Enscoe, Nicholas, Hart, Brag, Cooper, Thorpe, Holland Bake, and Miss J. SIMPSON, (Pupil of Mr. Le Clercq.)
The Fairy .... Miss J. SCOTT;   And Nerine, ... Mrs. LE CLERCQ.
Peasants ...... Master Conway, Misses M. Nichols, C, Bennet, Brock and Rountree, (Pupils of Mr. Le Clercq.)

IN THE COURSE OF THE EVENING, AN ENTIRELY NEW COMIC SONG CALLED
" 1818 WONDERS!" WILL BE SUNG BY MR. STEBBING.

The Evening's Entertainments to conclude with a New and Splendid Harlequinade, (partly from Milton's Masque of Comus,) with New and Extensive Scenery, Machinery, Mechanical Changes, Tricks and Metamorphoses, invented and produced by Mr NORMAN, called

MIDNIGHT REVELRY;
OR, HARLEQUIN AND COMUS.

The Music by Mr. CROUCH.   The Dresses by Mr SMITHYES and Mrs. CROSS.
Comus, *(an Enchanter,)* Mr. HOBBS, late of the Theatre-Royal, Haymarket.
Damon, *(an Enchanter,)* Mr. KIRBY.   Pan, *(afterwards Pantaloon,)* Mr. T. BLANCHARD.
Bacchus, *(afterwards Clown,)* Mr. NORMAN, of the Theatre-Royal, Covent-Garden.
Sabrina, *(Goddess of the Deep,)* Miss LEWIS.   Ariel, *(Spirit of the Air,)* Miss J. SCOTT.
The Lady, *(afterwards Columbine,)* Miss RUGGLES, late of the Theatre-Royal, Drury-Lane.
Fauns, Satyrs, Bacchanalians, Sylvians, Ariels, and numerous other Characters incidental to the Pantomime, by the rest of the Company.

The GRAND MARINE SALOON, designed and executed by Mr. SERRES, Marine Painter to His Majesty.
The Chorusses and Vocal Department, arranged by Mr. KEELEY, (late of the Surrey Theatre).
The Machinery and Mechanical Changes executed by Mr. LEWIS & Assistants.
Stage Manager, Mr. W. BARRYMORE.

Hartnell, Printer, Wine-office-court, Fleet-street; and Albion-Press, Southwark.

☞ The Proprietors, in order to meet the wishes and suggestions of many Noble Patrons and Friends, have appropriated the Lower Circles of Boxes as Dress Boxes. The accommodation of the Frequenters of the Upper Circle has also been paid particular attention to—a full and perfect view of the Stage is maintained—while the appropriation of a tastefully decorated Saloon, for the purpose of Refreshments, will, it is hoped, add to the general comfort.

Lower Boxes, 4s.   Upper Boxes, 3s.   Pit, 2s.   Gallery, 1s.
Doors to be opened at Half-past Five, to begin at Half-past Eight.
Places for the Boxes to be taken of Mr. GRUB, at the Box-Office from Ten till Four

. EXTRA PATROLES ARE ENGAGED FOR THE BRIDGE AND ROADS LEADING TO THE THEATRE, AND PARTICULAR ATTENTION WILL BE PAID TO THE LIGHTING OF THE SAME.

years to drain the site, they were nearly bankrupt before the building was erected.

Fortunately the Waterloo Bridge Company (hoping to increase the traffic through its toll-gate) rode to the rescue by putting up the cash to finish the job. Yet when the theatre (then called the Royal Coburg) finally opened, the area had turned into a teeming slum filled with factory workers, fish hawkers, and hookers. So to give its ribald, gin-swilling patrons what they wanted, its management staged mainly sultry melodramas.

Even Charles Dickens, no stranger to London's sordid low life, found the theatre revolting. "At each step up the staircase," he reported, "the warmth and stench increase, until by the time one reaches the gallery…the odour positively prevents respiration."

Desperately hoping to attract a better class of patrons, new owners installed such costly gimmicks as a two-ton mirrored curtain (in which audiences could see themselves) or sank money into major alterations. But soon, even those who purchased pricey pit seats fled when the boisterous gang in the gallery poured ale on their heads. By 1870, with an outdoor market surrounding the Old Vic, the district was one of London's worst.

A playbill from the third night of theatrical activity at the Royal Coburg Theatre, May 13, 1818.

An exterior view of the Royal Coburg in 1819.

Though the theatre was twice put up for auction, no one wanted it. Its doors were closed in 1880.

It was saved within months by a 45-year-old temperance reformer named Emma Cons who, for £1,000 a year, rented it in the name of the "Coffee Palace Association." Banning alcohol, musicals, and bawdy plays, she replaced them with coffee, magic-lantern shows, and concerts. Ten years later, having raised £17,000 from donations, she bought the theatre's freehold under the name of the Royal Victoria Hall Foundation—which managed its operations for the following 94 years.

In 1898, with Emma ailing, Lilian Baylis, her 23-year-old niece, agreed to help her run the Old Vic for a year. Lilian stayed for four decades. After Emma's death in 1912, Lilian took over with steely devotion. She introduced ballet, opera, and Shakespeare, under such eminent directors as Tyrone Guthrie.

Though wages were far less than those in the West End, a notable roster of young actors signed up. Soon they'd be known by their last names alone: Redgrave, Olivier, Gielgud, Guinness, Richardson, Laughton, Lanchester, Robson, Ashcroft, and Leigh. They soon got used to Lilian's eccentricities, such as scolding one cast for scurrying to a shelter during a World War I bombing raid, "If you have to be killed, at least die at your job."

After turning her beloved theatre into a world Mecca of Shakespearean drama, Baylis died in 1937—just four years before the Old Vic was *actually* hit during a bombing raid. Guthrie toured the company outside London until the theatre reopened in 1950. Yet 13 years later, the celebrated Old Vic Company was disbanded when the government-subsidized National Theatre directed by Laurence Olivier moved in.

When the subsidies suddenly stopped in 1981, however, the Old Vic's governors, stuck with a £380,000 deficit, were forced to sell.

Lilian Baylis, who brought the Old Vic to prominence by presenting Shakespeare for the masses.

Never make a promise you can't keep—we opened on
October 31, 1983.

Though it cost us more than $1 million to buy it, the theatre's total restoration cost another $3.9 million. After deciding that the most beautiful period of the Old Vic's architectural history was 1881, our London designers brilliantly restored the auditorium to that time.

We hung a huge banner near the theatre which read: "Lilian Baylis, you're going to love this. Honest Ed." And for the gala reopening on October 31, 1983, we ran

Welcome to the Old Vic!

airport runway lights down the length of Waterloo Road.

The opening production was the musical *Blondel* by Tim Rice, produced by Cameron Mackintosh. Sir Laurence Olivier himself gave the opening speech. And

Anne and I with the royal patron of the Old Vic,
Her Majesty Queen Elizabeth, the Queen Mother,
who was our guest on opening night.

the Old Vic's royal patron, the delightful Queen Mum, Her Majesty Queen Elizabeth, was our honoured guest that night. (Soon afterwards, she invited us to a reception at Clarence House.)

I was now, to my amazement, a patron of the arts in London as well.

GLENDA JACKSON

April 1984

Dear Ed,

I happened to be in the Old Vic for the first
time since it has been re-furbished on the
occasion of Sir John Gielgud's 80th birthday
reception. I am just writing to say thank
you for having done such a wonderful job –
the theatre is a jewel!

Hope you are all well,

Best wishes,

Sincerely,

Glenda.

U nlike the Royal Alex and Old Vic, our Princess of Wales Theatre has hardly enjoyed such a distinguished history—but it's staged some sensational shows.

The thought of building another theatre in Toronto first hit me in 1989, when Anne and I were in Russia as guests of the Gorbachev government. We visited the magnificent Odessa Opera House, and we both were smitten by its beauty.

I even told Russian officials that if they'd send their famous craftsmen from the Hermitage to build us an exact replica, I'd pay all the labour costs in hard currency. We even had an empty parking lot just west of the Royal Alex, I explained, to build it on. They were madly excited—but the negotiations dragged on so long that, before we even signed a deal, the U.S.S.R. collapsed.

Meanwhile in London, Cameron Mackintosh's production of the musical *Miss Saigon* had opened with the

Another type of royalty: Glenda Jackson, a queen of the theatre, took the time to drop me a line of congratulations.

biggest advance sale in West End history. Cameron and I had been friends for 14 years, ever since he brought his first production, *Relatively Speaking*, to the Alex. When I saw the electrifying response to *Miss Saigon*, I told Cameron we'd like to co-produce it, but he said our stage was too small.

Still, that parking lot wasn't! I thought we could put a temporary theatre on it to stage the show, then pull it down when it ended—until I found that *Miss Saigon* cost $10 million at the time just to mount it.

But then, as David pointed out, all the record-breaking musicals then—*Phantom of the Opera, Cats, Les Misérables*—were not only vastly expensive, but hugely visual productions on massive stages. So we decided to build a permanent theatre with the finest technical facilities in the world—together with one of North America's biggest stages.

On August 5, 1991, a giant backhoe rumbled into the lot and scooped up a huge chunk of asphalt. I told the crowd of 400 that the theatre would have 2,000 seats on the horseshoe-shaped orchestra floor and two balconies, with elevators rising from four underground parking levels.

I said the architect would be the award-winning Peter Smith. Glenn Pushelberg and George Yabu would design the interior, and the eminent abstract artist Frank Stella

We're willing to turn our hands to anything!
Here, we want to get started on our new theatre,
the Princess of Wales.

would create 18 original lobby murals as well as the auditorium's dome.

I also said it would be the first theatre built in North America since Toronto's O'Keefe Centre was erected 30 years before. It would also be the first to be funded by private money since the Royal Alex.

And finally, I said the world's hottest musical, *Miss Saigon*, would be staged in the world's most modern set-

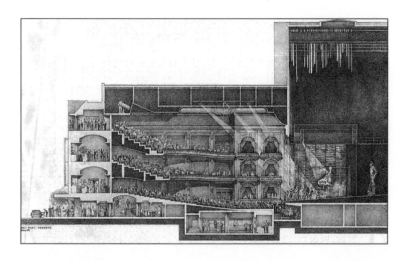

A cutaway showing the structure of the new theatre,
including the helicopter!

ting. And with that I introduced Cameron Mackintosh,
the man who'd produced 250 productions around the
world in the past 20 years. Then Cameron, Mayor Art
Eggleton, David, and I took gold-plated shovels and dug
the first holes.

The Princess of Wales cost $50 million to put up—in-
cluding the $20-million value of the land, the $23-million
construction cost, and $7 million in extra parking space.

The Mirvish–Mackintosh co-production of *Miss
Saigon* cost another $12 million to stage (as much as *Les
Miz* and *Phantom* combined), the greatest amount ever
spent on a show in Canada.

Miss Saigon, *the inaugural show at the Princess of Wales.*

Two happy guys at the official press opening
of our new theatre.

By opening night, the show had already run up $30 million in advance sales, the biggest in Canadian history.

The date of that opening, May 14, 1993, was auspicious. It was exactly 30 years since we'd restored and reopened the Royal Alex, and exactly 10 years since we'd bought and restored the Old Vic.

Among the 2,000 guests were Canada's governor-general, Ontario's premier, Toronto's mayor, the Metro chairman, prima ballerinas Karen Kain and Veronica

The original cast of Miss Saigon *take a bow at the premier: left to right, Melissa Thomson, Kevin McIntyre, Ma-Anne Dionisio, Kevin Gray. Melissa has done two other shows with us back-to-back since then.*

Tennant, "Saturday Night Live" producer Lorne Michaels, singers Michael Burgess and Salome Bey, comedians Frank Shuster and Don Harron, and most of the city's top dignitaries.

The thunderous curtain calls included ovations for Mackintosh and Miss Saigon's creators, Alain Boublil and Claude-Michel Schönberg, as well as David and me. I said, "Let the party begin."

For the gala post-show bash, we took over the giant abandoned Marine Warehouse at the foot of Jarvis Street and converted it into a palace—after adding 40,000 square feet of carpeting, 11,000 feet of pitch-black wall draping made of parachute material, two miles of electric cables for lights, 20,000 pieces of china, and 800 palm trees. A real helicopter also dangled from the ceiling, and the three-masted *Empire Sandy*, crammed with champagne bars, was docked at bayside.

The festivities ran on till 5 a.m., when breakfast was served. It was a fabulous opening, a fantastic show, a party not to be forgotten.

It looked like David and I were in the theatre business for keeps.

The first show I presented at the Alex was a comedy (though most critics disagreed) called *Never Too Late*. And it starred William Bendix— that gravel-voiced actor who looked like a boxing glove.

Though Bendix is best remembered for his long-running TV series, "The Life of Riley," and his character roles in such classic films as *Lifeboat*, *Detective Story*, and

Anne, David, and I point out some of the features of the theatre to William Bendix.

The Glass Key, the movie that made him a star was *The Babe Ruth Story.*

A die-hard New Yorker, he told me he'd grown up near Coogan's Bluff, which overlooked the Polo Grounds. In those days both the Giants and Yankees played the stadium, and Babe Ruth was young Bill's biggest hero. At 14, in fact, he realized his dream by becoming a Yankees bat boy—with the special task of keeping the Babe supplied in hot dogs, "which," Bendix grinned, "he could chomp down like Chiclets."

When the Depression hit, Bendix lost his job as a

grocery store manager and, with nothing else to do, studied acting. He then got parts in six successive Broadway flops. Depressed and broke, he was about to pack it in when he landed a key role in William Saroyan's hit, *The Time of Your Life*—which led to a call from MGM, and the subsequent lead in the Babe Ruth saga.

One night I asked Bendix what his biggest disappointment had been. Surprisingly, he snapped back, "The bloody *Babe Ruth Story*. When I got the part I was thrilled to death. When the shooting ended I was so upset I went into the hospital with ulcers. I literally wanted to die. It was a terrible, rotten movie.

"In fact," he emphasized, "every time I see a re-run on TV, I get sick all over again."

His outburst was so vehement I could only say, "Well, thank God, Bill, no one asked you to review it."

Over the decades, two shining knights of the theatre, John Gielgud and Ralph Richardson, have (as they say) trod the Royal Alex's boards in numerous plays.

Fortunately, they starred for us together in *No Man's Land*. On opening night I sat in my box straining to make sense of Harold Pinter's play—which, I'm ashamed to say, completely eluded me. When the curtain fell, I still didn't have the slightest inkling what it meant.

Backstage, I went to Richardson's dressing room and said, "Sir Ralph, please tell me, what was tonight's play all about?"

The actor turned and frowned at me for a minute. I felt myself shrink. Then, with the flicker of a grin, he said simply, "I don't know."

The next day I told my brother Bob, who was then a radio operator in the Merchant Marines, about this brief but bizarre exchange. Bob, who'd seen the show, said, "Ed, it's very simple. The play's like a ship that sails into port. The first thing the crew always does is gallop to the nearest bar. They sit and drink for hours till they're totally smashed. And then they begin to discuss serious matters. And every utterance sounds amazingly profound." Bob smiled. "The next morning, of course, no one remembers a single word anyone said. That's what Pinter's play's all about."

Backstage the following evening I told Richardson what my brother had said.

Sir Ralph frowned again, then nodded sagely. "Yes, Ed, that about sums it up."

To this day, I think both Bob and Ralph were putting me on. But I still haven't a clue what *No Man's Land* was all about. Someday, I want to ask Pinter.

A young man named Ronny Markowitz once worked for me in Honest Ed's. One day he told me he was quitting. He wanted to get into show business. I couldn't imagine what had possessed him, but I wished him well and he left.

In 1964, our second year at the Royal Alex, we'd booked everything from *My Fair Lady* to Josephine Baker—but still lacked a show to start the season off. One morning I was walking along King Street when a chauffeur-driven limo pulled up, and the guy in the back seat rolled down his window. "Hi, Mr. Mirvish, remember me?"

"Of course," I said, nodding, "you're Ronny Markowitz."

"Well," Ronny said, "I used to be—but I've changed my name to Randy Dandy."

I said it had a nice ring to it. And Mister Dandy was certainly catchier than Markowitz. Ronny-cum-Randy seemed pleased.

He invited me for lunch at a Japanese restaurant on Elm Street. It was, as I recall, named Lao Matsu, but Randy called it Lotsa Matzo. The waitress, fresh from

Osaka, brought us steamed cloths in a basket and lacquered bowls full of liquid. Randy instantly drained his bowl.

The waitress stifled her giggles behind her hand. The bowl, she said, was meant to wash your hands.

"I *know* that," Randy Ronny grinned back, "but I was thirsty."

The kid's chutzpah was infectious. I asked what he was doing. He said he'd just put together a new kiddies show and told me all about it.

So, despite the initial cocktail, the luncheon proved fortuitous for us both. Randy Dandy got to star on the Royal Alex's stage. And I was able to kick off our second season by staging his production of *Kidzapoppin* for a week.

But I've never eyed a fingerbowl since with any reverence.

When Red Buttons starred in *This Was Burlesque* at the Royal Alex, I found out he loved barley soup. So I took him to The Bagel on College Street. During lunch, I told him Anne and I had recently driven down the Pacific coast and saw

I wish Red Buttons could have seen me when I was
a mere 75 being serenaded at this birthday bash with the
cast of Les Miz.

a sign announcing Esalen. When the driver said it was a
famous nudist colony, I asked him to slow down. And
through the gates we could see the residents gardening
in the nude. "*Hold* it," I said, "this looks interesting."

Anne gave me a chilling glance. "Ed," she hissed,
"this is *not* for you." And told the driver to carry on.

Red laughed. "Ed, you won't believe it, but I drove
past Esalen with my mother once, and we did exactly the
same thing. Stopped outside, and stared at the nudists.
My mother didn't utter a word.

"Finally, she turned to me frowning, and said in Yiddish, 'You notice, son? There's not a single Jew in the joint.'"

On my eighty-second birthday, Red sent me a handwritten card which I've now got framed in my office. It says:

"Dear Ed, 82 is not old. Old is if you had season tickets to evolution.

"Old is if your parents sang you to sleep with Gregorian chants.

"Old is if you took a course in Shakespeare and Shakespeare taught it.

"Old is if you remember when career opportunities included shepherds.

"Old is if you have a personal letter from Columbus describing his upcoming cruises.

"*That's* old. Eighty-two ain't."

In 1965, Anne Corio starred for us in *This Was Burlesque*. Known as "The Girl with the Epic Epidermis," she was the favourite stripper of college students, as well as, she confided, the Washington diplomatic corps.

She told me she'd been in showbiz since 15, after winning a dance contest in her home town of Hartford, Connecticut. The first prize included a job in the chorus line of a Broadway show at $35 a week. "Getting the job was simple," Anne said. "Getting Mama's permission was something else."

Before agreeing, Mama Corio made a trip to the theatre in person, and got individual pledges from the manager, the entire cast, and backstage crew that they would each personally look out for the safety and welfare of her little girl. Only then, having got everyone's solemn vow, did Mama say okay. And Anne went to Broadway.

But a few days later, one of Mama's neighbours in Hartford said she'd heard little Anne was in burlesque.

"What you mean?" Mama asked in her thick Italian accent. "What's *burlesque*?"

Anne laughed when she told me. "Poor Mama had no idea. We'd never had burlesque in Hartford. We didn't even know the word."

But the neighbour swiftly filled Mama in, and the

description wasn't nice. She said it was just a notch above working the red-light district.

"And Mama," said Anne, "came back to the theatre like a shot. I almost fell off the stage when I went out to do a number and saw her sitting in the very first row.

"But after the show, she shoved her way backstage and said, 'Well, Anne, I guess is all right. As long as they look and no touch.'"

Over the years, they looked hard and long at the Queen of Strippers. Anne made big bucks and, she told me, invested them wisely in annuities, blue chip stocks, and real estate. She was also an officer of three large business corporations.

There was obviously far more to Anne Corio than an epic epidermis.

In 1966, we brought in the touring production of *The Owl and the Pussycat* starring Pat Suzuki. She told me it was her first legitimate show and she was thrilled to be in Toronto.

"The audiences seem so different here than anywhere else," she gushed. "In fact, everyone seems different."

When I asked what she meant, she said, "Oh, you know. Even the drunks here seem happy."

I agreed that indeed they were a jolly bunch.

We produced a lot of musicals in 1966. The Canadian cast was always the same, except for the leads, most of whom were American. One show was *Finian's Rainbow*, which starred Carmel Quinn and Bert Wheeler.

There was a particularly poignant moment in that play in which Carmel sang to Wheeler (who was then 75) on a bridge. But each time she finished her song, I noticed, Carmel jabbed the old man in his ribs.

After one performance I asked her why she did it. I said it didn't seem relevant to the scene.

"You're right," she said. "It's not in the script. But every time I sing that song, Bert falls sound asleep. I poke him to wake him up."

That same year I produced a new comedy by Eric Nicol called *Like Father, Like Fun.* Besides being a *Vancouver Province* columnist, Eric also wrote for TV and radio and had won the Leacock Medal for Humour. When his play ran in Vancouver, it had done extremely well with both the critics and the box office. I decided to try it out at the Royal Alex for six weeks.

The comedy was a hit in Toronto as well. And, since it was now my production, I decided to take it to Montreal for four weeks—then move it to Broadway. For a novice producer, I was beginning to see myself as Flo Ziegfeld.

When my plans were announced, I got a call from Nathan Cohen, the *Toronto Star*'s formidable drama critic. He told me, "The play is fine for Canada. It should also do well in Montreal. But if you take it to New York, they'll kill it. I'm not kidding, Ed. You're facing a massacre."

Well, Nathan knew his theatre (though countless actors and playwrights might disagree). But by then I'd been three years in the business and had presented dozens of shows. What did Cohen know that I didn't? Besides, I had to appease my ego. I wanted to prove myself on Broadway—and do it with a Canadian play.

So after Nicol's comedy made money in Montreal, I

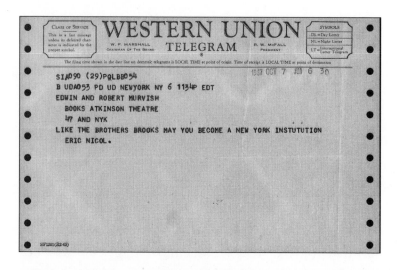

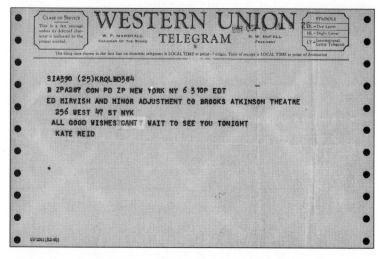

All the good wishes in the world, even from the playwright himself, Eric Nicol, and actress Kate Reid, couldn't save us from the massacre predicted by Nathan Cohen.

booked it into New York's prestigious Brooks Atkinson theatre. Then, on opening night, I waited for the raves.

I'm still waiting. The reviews were unanimously devastating. Massacre was an understatement. The show closed with a whimper in a week.

Yet, in fairness, I shouldn't say the critics were "unanimous." The famed columnist Walter Winchell actually liked it. I meant to call and thank him. But he died soon after the play did.

It took me months to face Nathan Cohen. When I did, I should have hired him.

The Eric Nicol play was not my only dashed dream of a Broadway hit. In 1981, we produced a musical called *Say Hello to Harvey*, planning to take it on to New York.

The show, I thought, couldn't fail. It was based on Mary Chase's celebrated comedy, *Harvey*, the play about an invisible rabbit that won the 1945 Pulitzer Prize and ran for 1,789 performances on Broadway—before becoming a Jimmy Stewart movie classic. The new musical's star was Donald O'Connor, and Leslie Bricusse wrote the music.

Mary Chase herself attended all the rehearsals and was at the Royal Alex on opening night. The unassuming wife of a Denver newspaperman, Mrs. Chase had been stunned by her play's initial success (with translations in a dozen languages, including Arabic, Japanese, and Hindi), and was anxiously looking forward to *Harvey's* reincarnation 36 years later.

She told me that the play's initial Broadway star, Frank Fay, had been married to film actress Barbara Stanwyck. But after a fiery marriage, they'd finally divorced in a storm of publicity. Soon afterwards, *Harvey's* eager press agent learned that Stanwyck was in New York.

He phoned her at the Pierre Hotel, Mrs. Chase recalled, and asked what night he could send her tickets to see *Harvey*.

"*Never*," Barbara Stanwyck barked. "I've seen all of Fay's damned rabbits."

Unfortunately, Stanwyck wasn't the only one who wanted nothing more to do with *Harvey*. Our musical version became so overblown (you couldn't move backstage for the sets) that both critics and audiences came away baffled. Though we managed to run for about six weeks, due mainly to O'Connor's manic presence, the show was a flop. There wasn't a hope of taking it to Broadway.

We dropped a bundle on *Say Hello to Harvey*. But at least I didn't come out of it completely empty-handed.

I've still got all of Leslie Bricusse's music for the show.

It's packed away somewhere in a trunk, beside an invisible rabbit.

You'd think I'd learn. I never do. Where's Nathan Cohen when you need him? When Darren McGavin starred in our hugely successful run of *The King and I*, he told me his wife, Melanie York, had written a terrific new comedy called *Fairytale*.

I read the script and liked it so much, I agreed to cut the last week of *The King and I* (if you can believe it) in order to try out Melanie's show. If it proved to be the hit we expected, I said I'd take it to Broadway.

Well, I might have liked *Fairytale*. And the McGavins might have loved it. But we seemed to be a minority of three.

Fairytale was a week-long flop.

Some critics even implied I'd lost my mind by ditching *The King and I* for what turned out to be The Egg and I.

Until they open, you rarely know which shows will pack the theatre. But one you could always count on was *Second City* from Chicago— which we brought to the Royal Alex annually.

Over the years I've seen hundreds of plays, but I rarely recall a line of dialogue. Yet I still remember the *Second City* skits (and explosions of laughter) that Avery Schreiber, Jack Burns, and Bob Dishy delivered at the Alex.

The show opened with a man in rags crawling painfully, snail-like across the stage. Finally, he reached a door on the other side. With his last ounce of energy, he reached up and feebly rapped. "Mother, father," he moaned, "it's your prodigal son. I've come home. Let me in."

The door suddenly swings open, and a huge gruff guy looks down and snaps, "They've moved," then slams the door in the prodigal's face.

In a final skit a husband comes home to find his wife in bed making wild love with a stranger. "Darling," he says drolly, "I guess the magic has gone out of our marriage."

You could take *Second City* to the bank.

The exuberant cast of Godspell. *Can you find the* Second
City *alumnae, Andrea Martin and Gilda Radner?*

Many of the greatest thespians of our age have
played the Royal Alex. But the finest, I've
found, regardless of their fame, consider
themselves not stars but seasoned actors.

When Rex Harrison arrived to play Pirandello's

Henry V, I learned the difference between actors and "stars." One clause in his contract demanded a chauffeur-driven limousine. Pricey, I thought, but no problem—until I finished the sentence, which read: "On standby, 24 hours a day."

What? I thought. Did Doctor Doolittle plan to eat, sleep, and perform in the limo's back seat?

Another clause insisted on a refrigerator in his dressing room—to be filled with champagne. Since we didn't have a dressing-room fridge, we got one and stocked it. Professor Higgins blithely accepted it as his due.

Finally (before the champagne and chauffeur bills gave our accountant a seizure) *Henry V* ended. En route to the airport, Rex told his bleary-eyed driver, "I'm aware I haven't tipped you, my good man. But there's a brand-new refrigerator in my dressing room worth a few hundred quid. It's *yours*."

The next day, Yale Simpson, the theatre's general manager, saw the driver lugging the fridge from the theatre. When stopped, the poor guy told him proudly, "Mr. Harrison gave it to me personally."

"That was extremely generous of him," Yale proffered. "But there's just one hitch. The refrigerator isn't *his*."

I met the same driver a few years later. He swore he hadn't chauffeured an Englishman since.

During the run of *Henry V*, a young man went to the stage door after a performance clutching a glossy photograph of Rex Harrison. Handing it to the doorman, he asked if the star would please sign it for him. The doorman said he'd see what he could do.

Ten minutes later the doorman returned and sadly handed the boy his picture. Instead of being autographed, it had been torn into shreds. The photo had shown Rex in a cardigan, and Harrison hated it.

In fact, the show's press agent had given us that very photo for publicity purposes before the show had opened. When Harrison saw it, he demanded we change it at once. I don't know if the press agent lost his job, but I do know Rex Harrison lost a fan forever.

One rotund Englishman the Anglophobic chauffeur never met was Robert Morley, the star of our play *The Picture of Innocence*. For an actor

He is the picture of innocence, isn't he?

who'd made a career of personifying petulance, I found him charming and vastly amusing.

The play, which Morley co-authored, was a comedy about transvestites, a trio of married men who liked dressing up in long, flowing gowns. "But then," as Robert noted, "so does the Pope."

Since the production was a world première, Morley was especially concerned about the critics. "Actually," he confided, "I'm prepared for any review. As long as it isn't headlined 'What A Drag.'"

Morley turned 70 during the run and told me he'd received a phone call from his son Sheridan, the distinguished theatre critic. The London papers had asked Sheridan how his father was celebrating his birthday. "He's in Toronto," said the dutiful son, "in a rather fetching cocktail dress."

Not long before, Morley had been the surprise guest on the TV program "This Is Your Life." He said he'd thoroughly enjoyed the experience. "Until the following morning, when I happened to run into Rex Harrison in Burlington Arcade.

"Rex shook my hand and said, 'Saw the show, old man. So brave. Allowing them to do that with your life. I'd never dare, what with all my ex-wives and different families. It's far too complicated. But then of course, Robert, you've always been so different than me. One wife. One family.' Then turning, he shot back over his shoulder, 'And, if I may say so, one performance.'"

Before *The Picture of Innocence* opened, Morley asked if I could provide him with a comfortable chair to sit in during his offstage intervals. It would save him trudging to his dressing room. So we got him a large expensive wing chair and placed it backstage. Morley was delighted.

On the night of the final performance, though, I asked one of our ushers to remove the chair. I knew from past experience that once the final curtain drops and the stagehands strike the set, *everything* in sight instantly disappears into trucks. So I took no chance of losing my valuable piece of antique furniture.

Robert didn't say a word, and I thought no more about it. A few months later someone sent me a clipping from the London *Observer*. It was an article written by Morley himself describing his sojourn to Toronto. The gist of the piece was nicely complimentary—until the end.

Morley concluded by describing "this character named 'Honest Ed' Mirvish, who owns and runs the

Royal Alexandra Theatre. Beware of men who call themselves honest. He loaned me a chair for my personal use for the run of the play. Then, even before the show had ended, Honest Ed pulled the chair right out from under me."

Looking back, I can appreciate Robert's pique. But, 20 years later, I still have my chair.

Trevor Howard was another famed British actor who played the Royal Alex's stage in *The Scenario*, the world première of Jean Anouilh's play in English. The action took place in a country inn outside Paris, and Trevor played an alcoholic director.

He certainly got into his part. My staff informed me that the star was never sober for a second, offstage or on.

Yet one thing was certain: as a drunk, Trevor Howard gave a stellar performance. Even the critics acknowledged that. His drinking never once hurt the play or his performance. It would have been fascinating to see how he'd have played it sober.

Still, we all agreed. Trevor was by far the most convincing lush we'd ever seen on stage.

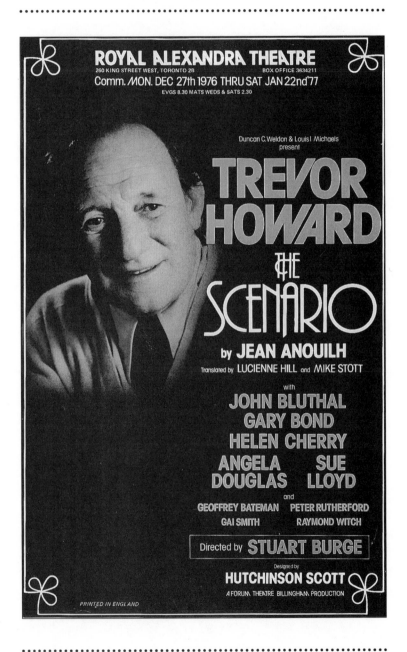

L arry Parks was the star of our hit comedy *Any Wednesday*. From what he told me of his life, I've always admired his grit.

He said he'd been studying medicine at the University of Illinois when he joined the drama club. By the time he got his degree, he was hooked by the stage and toured the midwest with an amateur theatre troupe.

Emboldened by the applause, he headed to New York where he instantly landed a job at Carnegie Hall—as an usher, at nine bucks a week. Undeterred, he wrote 64 letters to summer stock managers. From six replies, he accepted the job that paid the most.

Finally, after another shot at Broadway, Warner Brothers lured him west with a lead in the film *Mama Ravioli*. Larry was thrilled. Then, 36 hours before shooting was to begin, the movie was cancelled. By then Parks was broke. While waiting for another break, he took odd

Perhaps Trevor Howard's success in The Scenario *was due to the fact that he seemed to be able to maintain a constant state of drunkenness—the staff never saw him sober.*

jobs—such as reading lines with actors making screen tests.

One was with Barry Fitzgerald. Though Barry didn't get the part, Columbia was impressed with Larry and signed him to a term contract. He then appeared in more than 30 pictures before shooting to instant stardom in *The Jolson Story*, followed by *Jolson Sings Again*.

After Hollywood's Communist witch hunts, Larry Parks was one of the famous names blacklisted. For years, he couldn't get work.

With theatre, regardless of the lure of the spotlights and roar of the crowd, there's always a price to be paid. I remember once remarking to a director what a difficult, often agonizing business it was. He looked at me blandly and said, "No one ever promised you a rose garden."

Lauren Bacall, the blonde who taught Bogie to whistle, headlined our hit musical *Applause*. And the lady also had a special demand: baby-blue broadloom in her dressing room. Though it was as difficult then to find baby-blue broadloom as it must be now, I was happy to oblige.

After expressing her delight with the carpet, Lauren

gushed, "The babies will adore it." Unaware of any recent offspring on her part, I simply said, "I hope so."

Then she arrived with the "babies" in tow. Three small dogs—poodles as I recall. And they adored the broadloom to bits.

After opening night, as usual, we threw a party for the cast. One of our waiters poured Miss Bacall a glass of wine, then turned to the next table.

"*Waiter*," she growled in that voice of molten lava. "Just...leave...the...bottle...*here*." And he did. As he should have. Our stars (give or take the odd fridge) deserve star treatment.

As for that rug. By the time the show ended, it was no longer broadloom—or blue. We threw it in the trash.

Jack Carter starred in our production of *Guys and Dolls*. Hal Linden (who later become far more famous as TV's Barney Miller) and a young Canadian actress, Sandra O'Neill, also headed the bill.

I'll never forget the opening-night reviews. The critics mostly applauded the show, liked Linden, and raved about O'Neill—but almost ignored Jack Carter.

Jack was incensed. He charged up to me and stormed, "Dammit, Ed, I don't need this crap. I make more in one night in Vegas than I do in this joint all week."

"I'm sorry, Jack," I murmured, "but I didn't write the reviews."

He glared at me briefly, then nodded, "Yeah, you're right. But I'll get the bastards who did."

And every night for the rest of the show, right after the curtain call, Jack stepped onto the apron and told the crowd in implicit (but unprintable) terms what @#%$&*@ morons the Toronto critics were.

Though embarrassed for his victims (whom I'd still have to live with), I can't really say I minded that much. Our audiences got a second, impromptu, performance— which didn't cost me a dime.

Any Wednesday landed on the Royal Alex's stage with Britain's voluptuous June Wilkinson as its star. One Toronto paper announced her arrival as "44-20-36 Is Coming To Town."

Miss Wilkinson had become an instant sex symbol after baring all for American males in five separate issues of *Playboy* magazine. After this unprecedented exposure,

Hollywood embraced her. But after a couple of forget-table flicks, June wound up singing with Spike Jones's band.

When she came to Toronto, my visits with her were cordial but brief. In the back of my mind I could hear Anne's admonition ("Ed, this is not for you. Drive on."). Yet June was refreshingly frank.

She told me, "The first night I sang with Spike I wore a plunging gown. The applause was deafening. The next night, just to be different, I wore a frilly high-necked dress—like Grace Kelly in *High Noon*. From the lack of applause, I thought I was deaf.

"After that show, Spike came backstage and said, 'You better get back in that first dress, kid, 'cause you don't sing that good.'"

I n 1966, Sal Mineo first starred for us in *What Makes Sammy Run?* By then he'd graduated from his teenaged rebel roles with buddy James Dean to adult leads in *The Gene Krupa Story* and *Exodus*. He said he loved the part of Sammy Glick because as a boy he'd played the role himself.

"If I hadn't been such a bad smart-ass hustler as a

kid," he laughed, "I'd never have ended up acting." He told me he grew up with the street gangs in the Bronx. At nine, he said, he robbed a neighbourhood store—then hid the stash in one of his father's coffins.

"In his *what*?" I shot back.

"Yeah," he replied, grinning. "My dad was a casket maker. He opened it up to show a customer and discovered my stolen loot. I'll never forget my mother's lament. 'My Gaaaawd,' she shrieked, 'if Sal's stealing at nine, what will he be doing when he's *twelve*?'"

So they hauled him away off the street and stuck him in acting school. And soon he was appearing on stage in *The Rose Tattoo* and *The King and I*, before moving on to Hollywood—"where," he said, "you'll meet a Sammy Glick with his feet on the desk every time you walk into an office."

Sal Mineo was back at the Alex some years later appearing in a new drama based on the Manson murders. And the play indeed was rife with murders. The trouble was that during its opening week, the director kept changing the ending.

One night before the curtain went up, I found Sal

backstage in a seething rage, looking for the director. I asked him what the problem was.

"The *problem*?" he yelped. "The problem is that one night I'm supposed to kill the mother. The next night I'm supposed to kill the father. The problem is... who in the hell am I supposed to kill *tonight*?"

Britain's acting knights are an amazing breed. Some of them will tackle the most unlikely chores. For instance, in 1972, Sir John Gielgud directed a musical for us called *Irene*, with Debbie Reynolds in the lead.

Before one Saturday matinée, Miss Reynolds was stricken with laryngitis and came to me distraught. She didn't want her understudy to go on because, as Debbie pointed out, the audience had come to see Debbie. And, although she couldn't sing a note that day, she could still tap up a storm.

Over the years I'd always been told that the mellifluous Sir John could read the phone book and audiences would love it. Based on that, I half-jokingly suggested a compromise. Debbie would go out and do her big dance number on top of a piano, while Gielgud read her lyrics aloud from the wings.

Everyone thought it was a great idea. The audience would not only get to see the diminutive star in person, but they'd also get to hear the great Gielgud for free. It would be, we figured, a theatrical event so unique that patrons would later tell their grandkids.

We figured wrong.

I still don't know about the telephone book. I do know that when the patrons heard Sir John read Debbie's song, they walked out in droves. *And*, instead of hitting the street, *1,500 people* stopped at the box office to demand their money back.

Sheer disaster. I told the cast if it happened again, Debbie would tap dance in the wings while Sir John could go out atop the piano and spout Shakespeare.

But the world was spared that historic scene. Later that same night, miraculously, Miss Reynolds got her voice back.

Six years later, in 1978, John Gielgud was back at the Alex, this time starring in the play *Half-Life*. At the time he was 74.

One night he talked about theatrical technique, of which the aging knight was an acknowledged master.

He said he worked extremely hard to get every new role right, down to the tiniest detail—and had a horror of using old techniques that had proven popular in the past.

He said after World War II he was with a fine company, but noticed that some of the older actors often avoided inventiveness by patching their performances with clever bits they'd done in other plays.

He shook his head. "I would never do this. Every part demands the creation of a brand-new individual. The important thing is one's *vitality*. Vitality is the essential thing about voice, body, character, everything. If you lose vitality, you are lost.

"With every role you must force yourself into a new mental groove. And it should be more interesting *and* more difficult than anything you've done before."

Then he looked at me, and with his gentle smile said, "I'm sorry to bore you with an old man's musings."

John Gielgud couldn't bore you if he tried. His vitality is electric. Still, you might note, I never once asked him to read the phone book.

I n 1976, Katharine Hepburn played the Royal Alex in *A Matter of Gravity* during a bitterly cold January. To my amazement she insisted that the stage be kept at a nippy 50 degrees Fahrenheit. "But what about the patrons sitting in front?" I asked. "Surely they'll be cold."

"Don't worry, Ed," she reassured me. "*I'll* warm them up."

Well, she may have warmed their hearts, but she didn't thaw their bodies. I got letters from patrons who said if they ever came to the Alex again, they expected us to provide blankets.

T hat fabulous acting couple, Hume Cronyn and Jessica Tandy, played *The Gin Game* for us in 1979. They'd already done the show for 15 months on Broadway (where it won the Pulitzer Prize), taken it through the States, and were planning an international tour.

In it they played two alienated inmates of a home for the aged who become caught up in ritualistic games of gin rummy that come to mirror the unhappy rituals of their lives. The play was written by Don Coburn, a former Dallas ad man, whose previous big success was creating "The Pepsi Challenge."

Hume told me the play had first run in Louisville, and its producer had given him the script. Hume loved it and sent a copy to Mike Nichols in New York. Nichols called back the next day, suggesting they form a partnership to produce it on Broadway. He'd direct, and Hume and Jessica would star. It opened, of course, to rave reviews.

But the Cronyns changed the ending. "In the original script," Jessica told me, "Hume leaves me in despair. But on stage we both return to the card table. We insisted on that. The audience wanted it so much."

Hume called *The Gin Game* "hilariously funny. But what's at the base of the play is still bloody serious. The laughter isn't worth a damn unless the audience sees the emotional investment of these two desperately lonely people. The audience has to see their wounds."

At the time, the Cronyns had been married for 36 years. I was with them once when a reporter asked Hume if, during all that time, they ever considered divorce.

Hume turned a steely eye on the guy. "Divorce?" he snarled. "*Never!* . . . Murder? *Frequently!*"

When the reporter left, they both broke out howling.

"People seem to think we've discovered some golden formula for life," Hume explained, "and they want us to reveal it."

"Or else," said Jessica, "they want us to admit we're secretly miserable and really hate each other."

"It's a no-win situation," grinned Cronyn. "If we don't admit to either, people think we're simply dull."

Almost 15 years after *The Gin Game*, Anne and I met the Cronyns again. Jessica, who'd since won an Oscar for *Driving Miss Daisy*, was in Toronto making a movie, so I took them to see the Princess of Wales theatre just before it opened.

The young cast of *Miss Saigon* was in rehearsal then, and when they saw this legendary pair in the wings, the entire company erupted into wild applause. Hume and Jessica were obviously moved. I suddenly realized that the couple beside me, then nearing their eighties, had spent more years on stage than all the souls in the theatre combined.

To those hopeful bright-eyed actors, the Cronyns must have looked like icons, the epitome of every actor's dream. Still applauding, the cast ushered the couple on stage. Both Hume and Jessica pronounced the theatre gorgeous and said how much they'd love to play it.

Later, during lunch at Old Ed's with Anne, David,

and me, Jessica ordered stuffed trout from the menu. When the waiter asked if she'd like the head removed, Miss Tandy, ever the actress, announced, "Heavens no. Leave it on. I love the eyes looking at me."

In 1980, Cab Calloway and his famous Hi-De-Ho orchestra sailed into the Royal Alex with a show called *Bubbling Brown Sugar*.

On the day before they opened, Cab went to our box office and requested two tickets for that night's performance.

The week before, I'd just hired a smart Asian-born box-office manager whose grasp of English, I admit, wasn't up to his business savvy. The manager happened to be at the wicket when Calloway arrived. He handed Cab the two tickets, then said, "Seventy-two dollars, please."

"You don't understand," Cab told him. "I don't pay for tickets. I'm the star of the show."

The manager said, "Sorry, seventy-two dollars."

"Wait a minute," said Cab. "Do you know who Cab Calloway is?"

"Sorry," said the guy, "don't know of him."

Hi-De-Ho, Cab!

I was sitting in my office when Cab charged in. "For godsakes, Ed," he growled, "who's the idiot running your box office? He hardly speaks English, he never heard of Cab Calloway, and he wants to charge me for two tickets."

"Cab," I said, "that's why I have him in the box office. This guy doesn't know anybody."

Cab, to his credit, broke out laughing. And of course I gladly gave him his two tickets. Compared to chauffeured 24-hour limos, it was nothing.

The minute a show closes, as I've said, the backstage area is stripped in hours. Props, costumes, scenery, *everything* is cleared out—often including things that shouldn't be.

After one production, we suddenly discovered that an expensive stage light called a "follow spot" had disappeared. An intensive search failed to find it, and we finally decided someone had snatched it.

Soon after, I happened to mention the theft to an employee who worked in our Theatre Museum above Old Ed's, where the public can buy old theatre props and costumes. "Oh no, Ed," he told me, "the follow spot wasn't stolen. It wound up here in the museum."

Mystified, but delighted, I said, "That's terrific. I'll have someone take it back to the theatre."

"Well, there's just one problem with that, Ed," he said sheepishly. "It was sold two days ago."

Darned if we didn't have to buy it back.

But the Royal Alex's greatest unsolved mystery is the case of the missing undershorts. Before relating this Sherlockian opus, though, I must let you in on a little-known theatrical oddity: Actors on stage don't wear their own underwear.

Don't ask why. I've no idea. But the show's wardrobe people provide the underwear the actors must wear when performing. After each show, it is laundered. Then before the next performance, the fresh underwear and clean costumes are laid out on long tables in the theatre basement. The actors simply pick them up and take them to their dressing rooms.

For years this procedure ran smoothly—until an actor named Roger Bart came to the Alex to play Dickon in *The Secret Garden*. Every night (and twice on Wednesdays and Saturdays), Roger would go to pick up his costume. And everything was always there *except* his underwear. Wardrobe would give him a new pair of shorts. Roger would wear them and turn them in.

Wardrobe would launder them and lay them out. But Roger's briefs were *never* there when he arrived. Someone swiped them before every show.

We even had people watching the tables. But we never nabbed the panty raider. And never had a clue why it happened.

It would have driven Holmes to drink.

People ask if anyone ever toppled into the Alex's orchestra pit. Well, only one that I know of. But she didn't fall. She *jumped*.

In the play *One for the Pot*, the star Heath Lamberts, screamed around the stage in one scene spraying a seltzer bottle. Heath has a tendency to get excited when he's on. And patrons in the front row frequently got drenched (we paid the cleaning bills).

One night a woman in her finest Armani silk, sitting front row centre, saw Heath's stream of seltzer coming at her. And she *dove*. Right under the brass guard rail, into the orchestra pit, narrowly missing the conductor. A startled violinist said, "Well, *hellllo*, there," when he found her sprawled across his lap.

From that night on we called *One for the Pot*, One For The Pit.

Still, except for that swan-diver, no one to my knowledge has ever fallen into the pit—but a lot of things have. During the run of *Les Misérables*, an actor accidentally kicked one of the huge "paving stones" of Paris into the orchestra and beaned a musician. The stones were made of plastic, though, and the guy was only stunned.

But during the run of Jonathan Miller's absurdist comedy, *One-Way Pendulum*, we narrowly avoided disaster. The set for the play was built on the steepest rake I've ever seen. Downstage was really *down*, and walking upstage was like scaling a sloping ramp.

One of the stars was the great English character actress Betty Turner, who'd been performing for more than 70 years. Betty, then two years shy of 90, played an old lady in a wheelchair—who sat on stage for most of the first act.

She was wheeled on by another actress but had to pull the wheelchair's parking brake herself. I was terrified that one night Betty would forget to set the brake, and she'd hurtle downstage into the orchestra. So we had a safety net strung across the pit.

And a good thing too. Though 88-year-old Betty always remembered her brake, a 35-year-old stagehand forgot *his*.

One of the show's key props was an antique cast-iron weighing machine (the kind that spit out your weight and fortune for a penny), which weighed more than 500 pounds. It was wheeled on stage on casters, which were then locked—or *should* have been.

Just before the curtain, a stagehand rolled it on—and simply left it. It shot downstage like a runaway cannon, sailed into the pit, hit the net, then trampolined 10 feet in the air and landed on the brass guard rail separating the pit and the first row of seats.

The beautiful old brass work was smashed beyond repair. But no one was injured. And at least we knew our safety net could bounce off 500 pounds.

We never really worried about dear old Betty again. Minus her wheelchair, she weighed exactly 98 pounds, even with her greasepaint on.

Whe *One-Way Pendulum* opened, we'd just started our theatre company, Mirvish Productions, with a staff we'd mainly hired from small Toronto theatres.

One nice thing about people who've worked in small theatre companies is they haven't the remotest idea what "job description" means, since they're so used to doing anything that needs to be done. For instance, the new receptionist at Mirvish Productions, Stephanie Gorin, had done everything in theatre, including acting.

So, one morning, when *One-Way Pendulum*'s leading actress, Kathryn Pogson, was suddenly stricken with a throat infection, one of our new executive producers, Ernie Schwartz, tore upstairs to the head office.

Tossing Stephanie a script of the play, he panted, "You're off reception, kid. You've got to learn the part of Sylvia by eight...with a British accent, by the way."

And Stephanie did! She not only learned the part, but portrayed it (with accent) for a week. Fantastically. I'm sure the audience thought she'd rehearsed for months.

When Kathryn Pogson finally regained her voice, she

Our patrons don't hesitate to tell us what they like and don't like, and the absurdist farce One-Way Pendulum *was not to everyone's liking.*

went back on stage. And Stephanie, with exquisite grace, returned to the reception desk. Everyone at Mirvish Productions was overjoyed. For good receptionists are far harder to find than good actresses.

In the past 35 years, I've met every type of actor, but I still consider Stephanie Gorin one of the true stars. I always thought she'd go on to pursue a brilliant acting career, but Stephanie surprised us all. Instead, she became a superb casting director. And we've hired her talents many times since for major productions ranging from *Les Miz, Miss Saigon, Crazy for You*, and *Jane Eyre* to, most recently, *Rent*—the hit Broadway musical that had the biggest first-day ticket sales (grossing more than $500,000) in the Royal Alex's history.

When I call Stephanie Gorin a "true star," I should explain. To me the expression entails not just celebrity, but outstanding ability. True stars bask more in applause than their

She may have been looking in the universe for intelligent life, but Lily Tomlin is the kind of down-to-earth star I admire.

celebrity. Some of the greatest are down-to-earth people.

When Lily Tomlin starred at the Alex in *The Search for Signs of Intelligent Life in the Universe*, I overheard an interview in which a rather imperious reporter said to her, "Professional funny people aren't funny always." Then asked, "Are you funny?"

"I don't think I'm funny," Lily said. "I think I'm kinda wholesome. All my friends are so funny and amusing, I'm kind of like an innocent among them."

When told she'd "done a brilliant show," she frowned. "Don't say I was brilliant. I constantly work on my performance. That's part of the fun of it. I don't get bored because I think of new things to do."

But funny she is. She said she didn't mind being called an actress, "although I prefer actor because it sounds generic. Actress is like saying authoress. But I'll make an exception for waitress. I've been one. Lots of times. I waitressed at the Howard Johnson at 49th and Broadway, the one that's closed now."

She looked at the reporter with wide, innocent eyes, her expression almost plaintive. "Can you believe they'd shut it down—knowing that I'd worked there?"

WhEN we staged Neil Simon's *The Odd Couple*, George Gobel played the fastidious Felix and Phil Foster played Oscar the slob.

Phil's wife sat beside us on opening night. During the performance she turned and whispered, "Phil's not acting."

Puzzled, I murmured back, "What do you mean?"

"He really *is* a slob," she said.

ThERE was something particularly felicitous about Sir Peter Hall's company moving into our Old Vic Theatre in 1997. It was a return to the type of repertory, a mixture of new and classic plays, that made the Old Vic a byword for quality shows. The type of program, in fact, originated by Lilian Baylis.

There's no other theatre in London whose history is more imbued with the character of one person. For Lilian Baylis, stern and puritanically religious, ran the Old Vic from 1912 right into the 1930s, and made it the première theatre of Great Britain.

The Old Vic's very spirit was embodied by this irritating, unmarried, God-intoxicated, bespectacled woman who hardly ever watched a play through to the final curtain. Yet Lilian Baylis probably exerted a more profound influence on the performing arts in Britain than anyone else this century.

She did it from her tiny office in the theatre she loved and seldom left, far from the West End's mainstream. It's not an exaggeration to say that without her instinct, passion, and zeal, there would be no National Theatre, Royal Ballet, or English national opera, nor would English acting have acquired the international reputation it enjoys today.

I've been told she once prayed, "Lord God, send me a good actor, but send him cheap." Lilian was notoriously stingy with money, but generous with art.

She didn't seem to care that patrons would catch their heels in the holes in the carpets, as long as there was quality on stage—which she left (and expected) her superb directors to produce. And they did.

The joy and prestige of appearing at the Old Vic induced the greatest actors to accept miserably low wages. She treated everyone the same. There were stars only in Lilian's heaven.

When Robert Atkins, one of the leading actors in the company, advised her to go see what was happening in other theatres, Baylis sniffed, "Not keen on plays, dear. Don't know what they're about."

After watching some of the plays we've staged, I've sometimes shared her sympathies.

Long before I ever bought the Old Vic Theatre, I'd heard great stories about it from such English stars as Richardson, Gielgud, and Peter O'Toole. Peter received his early training on its stage and had wonderful memories of the place. But he said when he finally returned to star as Hamlet, "the reviews were so devastating, people actually came *just* to see how bad I was. And the bloody show became a *hit*."

Richardson loved telling Lilian Baylis stories. "Frugal to a fault," Ralph called her. "She ran a ship so tight it squeaked." He said one of Lilian's impoverished young actors approached her one day and asked if she could give him a little more pay. He said he couldn't live on his meagre salary.

"Lilian listened icily to his request," Sir Ralph intoned, "then told him to remain on stage while she retired into her office to confer with God.

"The poor boy waited half an hour before Lilian returned. Then, fixing him with an icy eye, she said, 'God...says...*no*.'"

*The Old Vic, all lit up and ready for
a wonderful night of theatre.*

Gielgud, who'd been listening, laughed. "Such an amazing, eccentric woman. Did you tell Ed about her accident?"

"Oh, *that*," chuckled Richardson. "Well, after putting the Old Vic on its feet, Lilian acquired the Sadler's Wells theatre, of which she was equally proud, to produce opera and ballet.

"Then one night, in front of the Old Vic, a woman was struck by a car. Someone in the crowd exclaimed,

My stage debut at the age of 80 as I celebrate my birthday with the cast of Crazy for You.

'My God, it's Lilian Baylis of the Old Vic.'
"With which the old girl, though seriously shocked, croaked back from the pavement, '*And* the Sadler's Wells.'"

D uring the run of *Crazy for You* I turned 80. As a birthday present, the cast asked me to appear for one performance—playing a backstage doorman in one scene.

Talk about stealing the show! Barbara Hamilton was a regular performer at our theatre, and she knew a thing or two about stealing a scene, if not the whole show. She had great fun as Lady Catherine de Bourgh in Pride and Prejudice, *here with Douglas Campbell as Mr. Bennett.*

When I appeared, the full-house audience rose en masse to give me an emotional two-minute ovation. Though deeply touched, I didn't know what to do. So I simply stood there.

Then the show went on with its razzle-dazzle, with me surrounded by the chorus girls.

Afterwards, a reporter asked the late Canadian actress Barbara Hamilton, who was in the cast, what she

The best way to turn 80—
surrounded by a froth of chorus girls.

thought of my performance. "I just wish Ed would let the
actors do the acting, and stick to his job as a storekeeper—instead of stealing the whole damn show."

Barbara was joking, of course. At least she said she
was. But that doorman's role was the beginning and end
of my acting career. No one's asked me to perform since.

On my 82nd birthday in 1996, I was honoured by the City of Toronto by being the first person to have a star implanted in the entertainment district's new "Walk Of Fame," stretching two blocks along King Street. The star sits in front of the Royal Alex theatre.

At the official unveiling attended by dignitaries, a few of our various stars sang—Michael Burgess and David Cassidy, who were appearing in *Blood Brothers*; Gail Bliss, who was starring in *Patsy* (the Patsy Cline story); and Chuck Wagner, who played the beast in Disney's *Beauty and the Beast*.

Chuck was supposed to sing the Beast's hit number in the show, "If I Can't Love Her," with the backing of a digital audio tracker. On cue, Chuck belted into the song. But the recorded music that boomed out was from another number in the show, "Be Our Guest."

Chuck Wagner couldn't believe it. Still, like a true pro, he bravely carried on—simply singing louder to drown out the clashing soundtrack. He felt humiliated at the end, but the crowd understood. They gave him a thunderous ovation.

When it came time to unveil the star in its granite block, I said the only higher honour the city could pay me would be, upon my final departure, to set the granite slab on edge.

"Just think," I said. "It would make a fabulous headstone."

Right after I bought the Royal Alex, David "Buddy" Lloyd became our property manager. Which means that almost everything you saw on stage, Buddy either bought, rented, or created—and then fondly looked after.

His backstage office was crammed with props and mementoes from hundreds of shows. In a place of honour on the wall hung a photo of actress Elaine Stritch. For, in all the years he'd been with us, Buddy appeared on stage only once. And Elaine was responsible for his short burst of stardom.

It was during the run of *Annie Get Your Gun*. Elaine, starring as Annie Oakley, was supposed to race a motorcycle around the stage while shooting at a target. The big bike was attached to a pivot that kept it going in a circle.

But suddenly the mechanism broke, and the bike just kept on rotating. Somehow Elaine managed to jump off. Yet then, unsure what to do, she simply stood there blasting blindly at the target—as the riderless bike kept roaring around her.

Because it ran right to the edge of the stage, it was impossible to close the curtain. That's when the boys in the orchestra pit started diving for cover. It's also when Buddy sprang into action, making his dramatic stage debut by racing out in full view of the audience to shut the mechanism down.

Of course he got a standing ovation.

But that one brief shining moment in the spotlight, he said, was more than enough. "I'll never go out on that stage again," he told me, "unless the house is empty."

Buddy Lloyd was one of a backstage trio committed to a firm belief that, whatever mishap might occur, the show would go on—if left to them.

Vic Ecclestone, our chief carpenter, spent his entire career at the Royal Alex until his death in 1997. Vic's dad had also worked at the theatre, as does Vic's son, Blair Ecclestone, today.

Mitch Wywiorski was our head electrician from 1971, until the O'Keefe Centre lured him away.

But together, the three were formidable. Their tiny office, about 20 feet offstage, was a cross between a crowded bed-sitter and a museum. It was furnished with cast-offs of past productions whose accumulation began before the trio ever arrived on the scene.

Opposite a gaudy if broken-down couch was a hot plate, sink, and huge refrigerator—for Buddy's edible props. From the ceiling hung such souvenirs as the shoe-stilts from *Equus*, an eagle from *Grease*, a voo-doo doll from *Don't Bother Me, I Can't Cope*, and cocked hats from *The Pirates of Penzance*.

The men had a story for each memento and production. Buddy would point to a laden cocktail tray used in the play *Half-Life*. Each night he'd wait off-scene to take it from the butler, and said he learned the actors' lines so well he could have stood in for any of them.

Besides concocting fake Manhattans from iced tea, he said one of his biggest challenges was finding a non-allergenic clay for the mud-slingers in *Hair*. During that long run, he recalled with disgust, his crew filled seven garbage bags each night with "feathers, mud, and general muck."

Vic would proudly show backstage guests a great ivy-covered stone wall he'd created—which in fact was made of plywood, plaster, and canvas, draped with spray-painted cloth.

And Mitch would gleefully demonstrate how, with the flick of a switch, he could alter dazzling Mediterranean sunlight into a night of flashing lightning. "What the audience doesn't see," he said with a grin, "doesn't matter."

The magnificent Bea Lillie. Unlike many professional comedians, she was funny both on stage and off.

The team took as much pride in averting disaster as they did in their technical miracles. Like the time they grabbed a boy delivering coffee just as he started to cross the stage in the midst of Gielgud's major speech in *Half-Life*.

Or, when the furniture for *The Last of Mrs. Cheyney* was stolen as it sat outdoors to be loaded, they tracked down the culprits and recovered each piece. Or, when a sprinkler pipe burst and drenched the actors in a sudden on-stage Niagara, they had the pipe repaired and every costume dried in time for the Act II curtain.

Yet, with the pressure of each performance, the trio had little personal contact with the casts. It didn't matter if it was Gielgud or an extra, the performers to them were just part of the overall production. "No matter who's acting," as Vic once said, "we just go ahead."

All three were dedicated to perfecting fantasy. And that they did superbly.

L ady Peel was born at 68 Dovercourt Road, Toronto, on May 29, 1898. She was known at the time, though, as Beatrice Lillie.

Tiny, gracious, and truly a lady, I've been told, she

became one of the great stage comediennes. She played the Royal Alex in 1936 in a play called *At Home Abroad*, and again in 1949 in *Inside U.S.A.*

British actors who knew her loved to regale me with Bea Lillie stories. Like the time she went with some of her chorus girls to have their hair styled at Elizabeth Arden's in London. In one of the adjoining seats was a snobbish dowager from the Armour Meat Packing family, who sniffed, "If I'd known that actresses and chorus girls frequented this salon, I would not have come."

Bea eyed her, but said nothing. Upon leaving, however, she audibly announced to the manager, "You may tell the butcher's wife that Lady Peel has finished."

There was also the time she arrived in a cab at London's Savoy Hotel with her pet Pekinese, Mig Ki Poo. Unfortunately, during the trip, the Peke had piddled in the taxi.

When the driver opened Bea's door and noticed the stain he snorted, "Missus, your dog's gone and peed in my cab."

Bea pressed a handsome tip in his palm. Then, just before sweeping through the grand hotel's doors, she announced in her haughtiest Lady Peel trill, "Not so, my good man. *I* did it."

In 1987 we opened our subscription season with *Three Men on a Horse*, George Abbott's classic comedy of horses and horseplay. The play was extremely appropriate. For this was the Royal Alex's eightieth season, and Abbott's one hundredth birthday.

Over the years the prolific playwright had given the world such perennial hits as *Wonderful Town, Call Me Madam, The Pajama Game, Fiorello!, Brother Rat*, and *Damn Yankees*—and was still, after a century, going strong.

That same season, we produced another of Abbott's musicals, *Pal Joey*. While discussing the play's opening on the phone, Abbott told me that four years before, at age 96, he'd had a pacemaker put in. He said he was feeling good about it until his doctor told him it was only good for 10 years and would then have to be replaced.

"What?" yelped Abbott. "You mean in ten years I'll have to go through all this *again*?" We both laughed.

But in fact, 10 years later, the old rascal *did*. He got his second pacemaker at 106—and wore it for a year before he died.

There's a story about the Royal Alex few people know. In fact, it's about a man hardly anyone remembers.

His name was Lawrence Solman, but everyone called him "Lol." He was born to poor Jewish immigrant parents (with which I identify already) on John Street, just around the corner from where the Alex now stands.

By the 1890s, Lol owned Hanlan's Point Hotel on the island, Hanlan's Point Amusement Park, the Maple Leaf's baseball club, and co-owned the Toronto Island Ferry Service. They soon called Solman "Toronto's Weekend King."

In 1906 he was one of the consortium of local businessmen who backed Cawthra Mulock's grandiose plan to build "the finest theatre on the continent." Which, of course, became the Royal Alexandra. And the board unanimously elected Lol, as the only member with any showbiz savvy, to manage it.

Lol, however, was hesitant to accept. Roller coasters and curveballs, he knew about. "But when it comes to legitimate theatre," he confessed, "I'm hardly a legit choice."

Yet manager he became. And even before the Royal Alex opened, he found himself in a life-and-death struggle with the notorious "Theatrical Syndicate." This was the powerful New York–based booking monopoly for North American touring shows, which had a financial stake in the elegant Princess Theatre just east on King at the corner of York.

The Syndicate, fearing Cawthra's competition, vowed to crush the upstart venture by blacklisting its shows— and turn the Royal Alex into "a carriage stable" for the Princess Theatre's posh patrons.

But Solman shrewdly won the battle by creating his own production company, The Royal Alexandra Players, and his own booking agency, Trans Canada Tours.

He also cleverly forged alliances with such other independents as the Shuberts and producer David Belasco. At the time, Belasco was offering a big new show called *The Warrens of Virginia* written by William C. de Mille, with a cast of 17. But the Syndicate's theatres wouldn't even consider it, because of its whopping $5,000 production cost.

Lol Solman, however, welcomed the play, which opened to sell-out crowds at the Alex in January 1909. Among the cast was the playwright's brother, a skinny young actor named Cecil B. de Mille. And the ingénue was that pretty Toronto girl, Gladys Smith—who, for the first time with this play, used the stage name Mary Pickford.

Solman's war with the Syndicate abruptly ended with a pair of events that coincidentally occurred on the same fatal night in 1916: the Princess Theatre burned to the ground. And a German U-boat torpedoed the *Lusitania*, bringing down the final curtain on the Syndicate's leading producer, Charles S. Fruhman, who bubbled to the bottom with the ship.

Still, it was chiefly through Lol Solman's efforts that the Royal Alex not only survived, but flourished. And today, amazingly, his name is all but unknown.

He died in his sleep in Wellesley Hospital on March 24, 1931. And his funeral, ironically, since Lol was hardly Protestant, was held at St. Andrew's Presbyterian Church, just across the street from the Royal Alex.

The reason, I discovered, is that once, when the church was undergoing major renovations, Solman invited the St. Andrew's congregation to use the theatre on Sundays. The grateful minister asked the Solman family for the honour of conducting St. Andrew's first and only Jewish funeral.

Two hundred cars followed the hearse to the cemetery. It was the longest funeral cortège ever seen till then on Toronto's streets.

After Lol Solman's death, the Alex was managed from 1939 to 1962 (the year I bought it) by a man named Ernest Rawley. Because of his close association with Lol, he was quite familiar with the theatre's operation, and during his 24-year tenure was greatly responsible for its continued success.

When Rawley took over, Solman had been dead for eight years, and the Alex had seriously declined. During the 1938–39 season, the theatre was open for only 15 weeks. But in Rawley's first five years of management, he had it running for 50 weeks a year, always with legitimate shows.

At the time it set a record equalled by no other Canadian theatre.

Since we renovated and reopened the Alex, I'm delighted to say, it's been running consistently for 52 weeks a year.

David and I with Diana, the Princess of Wales.

W hen we announced at a Toronto press conference that we were naming our newest theatre "The Princess of Wales," many people were surprised.

Because of the Mirvish family's long commitment to theatre, a lot of people (who'd forgotten my celebrated humility) asked me why it didn't bear the Mirvish name.

Well, I said, the enormous popularity of Princess Diana was definitely a factor—as was her well-known work with children and the elderly and her courageous public position on the care of AIDS patients.

I was a great admirer of Princess Diana, whom I met when she attended a performance of *Les Misérables* in 1991 at the Royal Alexandra. What struck me the most about her was her ability to connect with ordinary people on a personal level. She made everyone around her feel at ease. Although it was close to midnight when the play finished, she didn't make a beeline for her waiting car, as some celebrities would. Instead, she stopped to talk to the legions of people who had lined up for hours outside the theatre to catch a glimpse of her. It seemed to me that she had a private word with each person who was waiting. This was her special gift.

I last heard from Princess Diana earlier this year, when she sent me a letter to mark my 83rd birthday. Sadly, she died just a few weeks later in that tragic car accident in Paris. In the days following her death, mourners from all over left flowers, notes, and other mementos outside the Princess of Wales Theatre. It gave me some comfort to think that people had come to view the theatre as a monument to Diana's memory, and I'm sure she would have approved of the building had she lived to see it.

The name of the Princess of Wales also links it to its sister theatre, the Royal Alexandra. Because, in the past

When Princess Diana died tragically at 36, mourners spontaneously left flowers and other mementos at the theatre that bears her name.

150 years, there've been only three princesses of Wales. Alexandra of Denmark, for whom the Royal Alexandra was named, became Princess of Wales in 1863 when she married Queen Victoria's eldest son, Albert Edward.

When Alexandra became Queen in 1901, the title passed to Mary of Teck, wife of the future George V. It wasn't until 1981, when Prince Charles married Lady Diana Spencer, that there was again a Princess of Wales.

KENSINGTON PALACE

I am delighted to be associated with a project which, I am confident, will be of great importance to the City of Toronto, a city of which I have many fond memories.

I am equally delighted to have the opportunity to contribute to the continuation of two theatrical traditions. First, this theatre is the newest member of a family of royal theatres linking Britain and Canada. The Old Vic of London and The Royal Alexandra of Toronto are now joined by The Princess of Wales. Second, this theatre in its name links us to Toronto's past in its commemoration of the long-gone Princess Theatre which once stood three blocks to the east of this site.

I send my warmest congratulations to all those associated with the creation of this marvellous building and hope that it will bring years of enjoyment to the people of Toronto.

Diana.

January, 1993

We received this letter from Princess Diana in 1993, when we named our newest theatre in her honour. It was her warmth and generosity that people loved. She truly was "the people's princess."

In January 1993, we received a charming letter bearing the Kensington Palace coat of arms which begins: "I am delighted to be associated with...the newest member of a family of royal theatres linking Britain and Canada." It is simply signed "Diana."

As Diana's letter points out, both the Royal Alexandra and Princess of Wales theatres share a third sister, London's Old Vic, named for Princess (later Queen) Victoria. All three are "royal theatres," bearing royal names. And why is *that*?

Because in the seventeenth century, Oliver Cromwell's governing Puritans (who'd just beheaded the King) considered theatre an abomination. Though they didn't mind dancers, musicians, and jugglers, they considered "play acting" (in which actors pretended to be other than what God made them) a sin. So they tore down or burned almost every playhouse in England.

But after the Puritans fell, and people starting putting up theatres again, King Charles II instituted a restriction. To build a theatre for staging plays, you needed royal approval. If you got the King's licence (and you can bet it cost), then your theatre would be known as a "royal" or "legitimate" theatre.

Thus, the Old Vic, Royal Alexandra, and Princess of Wales are direct descendants of those old "royal" theatres, and we still use the term "legitimate" to distinguish them from concert halls, cinemas, and variety theatres.

Though the legal meaning of royal licences ended 200 years ago, a royal name remains a symbolic link with theatre history. But even today, you must still petition the Crown for permission to give a royal name to a theatre. And it isn't lightly given.

J ust imagine what Cromwell's theatre-burning bunch would have done if they'd seen our opening of *Hair* in the sixties.

Hair, of course, was the first musical to flaunt not only obscene language but frontal nudity—and, when I think about it, one of the last. In the free-love, flower-power mind space of the sixties, however, *Hair* was a huge theatrical hit—particularly with liberally minded sophisticates.

Our head maintenance man at Honest Ed's went to see the show with his wife. Though conservative in nature and not an avid theatre-goer, he always tried to see the "big ones." The next day he said he enjoyed the show, except when the cast sang "Age of Aquarius."

Almost every night at this point, the audience usually

stood and started swaying in rhythm to the music. But when someone behind him jostled our maintenance man and told him to join in, he turned around and snapped, "F— off, and quit pushing."

When I asked what happened, he shrugged. "Nothing. They seemed to think my line was in keeping with the show."

I was much more concerned with my mother's reaction to the play's language and nudity. When I asked what she thought of it, she slowly shook her head. "I just can't believe," she said, "how *hard* those kids work."

There's another quote I remember about *Hair*, which came from a fireman. But first, I have to emphasize that I have nothing but respect for Toronto's fire fighters. Over the decades they've given us spectacular service and have saved the lives of many of our patrons who've suffered heart attacks and seizures.

One day soon after *Hair* opened, a fireman came to our box office asking for tickets. He had relatives coming to town who were dying to see the show. The only problem was, during *Hair's* first months, every seat in the house was sold.

When he got the bad news, the guy said, "Hey, can't you give me a break? I'm with the fire department."

"Sorry," he was told. "We're completely sold out."

The guy went bananas. "Well, I'll tell you one thing, pal," he growled, before stomping off. "If you ever need to put out a fire here, you'd better be prepared to piss on it."

I know the fireman was understandably upset, but I still think there are better ways to douse a blaze.

Amazingly, even in the sixties, I was surprised how little puritanical outcry there was about *Hair* in "Toronto the Good." In 1930, the unclad cast would have been tarred, feathered, and galloped to jail on a rail.

That's the year J.J. Shubert, the king of Broadway producers, brought *Artists and Models* into the Alex, with seats selling from $1 to $3. The show was one of the musical revues Shubert had staged annually since 1923—each distinguished by its devoted display of female flesh. But when it hit Toronto, the censors went berserk.

As soon as Shubert heard they were trying to ban his production, he took the first train north. On arrival, the fuming J.J. told the critics there wasn't a single scene in the show to which any adult could take offence.

"But," retorted the censor board, "what about children who might see it?"

"Ahhh," Shubert reportedly replied, "that's why we set the ticket prices so high. No kid could possibly afford one."

The show continued to run.

I've never been interested in gambling, whether it's card games, the races, lotteries, or the stock market. But when I got into theatre, I found it the biggest gamble of all. Over the years, in picking shows I've taken some extremely long shots.

In the business world, I make no claim to any special expertise. I go with intuition—a feeling for what I think people want. I'm also attracted to the unknown and untried. And the same is true with theatre.

For instance, to open our 1979 subscription series, we had booked a play called *Waters of the Moon* for a month. Since it starred Ingrid Bergman, we were certain of success. But just before it opened, Miss Bergman had to cancel the tour.

Fortunately, the Royal Alex has a high priority with producers. Besides the sophistication of our audiences and the theatre itself, they also appreciate the fact that they leave town with a profit. So, when they heard we had a four-week gap to fill, we were offered five other shows.

Four were revivals of established hits. The fifth was a big new musical called *Home Again*, which had never been staged. Its producers wanted to try it out in Toronto before taking it to Broadway.

I knew the mortality rate for new musicals that year was already appalling. Among the Broadway disasters that had each lost up to $1.5 million were:

Platinum: Starring Alexis Smith; closed in New York.

A Broadway Musical: Closed after one night.

Les Girls, Les Girls: Starring Cyd Charisse and Tony Martin; never reached New York.

Back Country: A musical version of *Playboy of the Western World*; folded in Boston prior to Broadway.

Broadway, Broadway: Folded in Philadelphia.

King of Hearts: Closed in New York.

Grand Tour: Died on Broadway.

Whoopee: Closed in Washington.

That was the situation when I had to decide on one of four established winners or another big musical no one had seen. So what did I pick? The musical, of course.

But it wasn't all based on intuition. The people who'd

created *Home Again* were hardly slouches. The script was by Russell Baker, the hilarious *New York Times* columnist. Broadway veteran Cy Coleman had written the music. Tony Award winner Gene Saks was directing. Onna White, who'd won an Oscar for *Oliver*, was choreographer. And the cast included Dick Shawn, Ronny Cox, and Mike Kellin.

A gamble? Of course! But with a gang like that, I said, you can't go wrong. And thank God, I was right. *Home Again* played to packed houses.

In 1965 that amazing American impresario Sol Hurok brought the Polish Mime Theatre to the Alex on its first North American visit. Hurok was always heading behind the Iron Curtain to emerge with some sensational group or company in tow.

Before the show opened, I asked Sol how he managed to pull off such coups.

Spreading his arms he said, "Ahhhh, it's simple, my friend. This show is like most of them. I'd heard some fine things about it, so I flew to Warsaw to see for myself. I went to the theatre, and liked very, very much what I saw.

"So when it was over, I immediately went backstage

and made them an offer. They accepted. And that's it! You see, Ed, it's all very simple."

Of course, I saw. And it was very simple. Sol made them an offer they couldn't refuse.

One of the highlights of our 1968 season was the debut of a brand-new company called Theatre Toronto, which staged four plays in a two-month period.

The opening night was also the debut in English of Montreal critic Jean Basile's play, *Joli Tamboor*, which ran at the Alex as *The Drummer Boy*. It starred John Colicos and Richard Monette (as the drummer boy) and had one of the world's foremost directors at the time, Clifford Williams.

Williams came to Toronto with a list of amazing achievements behind him. At 40, he'd been associate director of England's Royal Shakespeare Theatre. He'd directed for Olivier's National Theatre at the Old Vic, staged *The Flying Dutchman* at the Royal Opera House, and directed Shakespearean productions for the Finnish National Theatre.

He'd also done *Volpone* at the Yale Drama School, put

on numerous comedies in London's West End, and produced command performances for England's Royal Family as well as for U.S. President Lyndon Johnson.

I was impressed. Especially when Williams said the new Theatre Toronto group was one of his greatest challenges. He told me he wanted to build a rep company here that would be recognized around the world. I eagerly awaited his first play.

It wasn't what I expected. *The Drummer Boy* was riddled with violence and perversity. In one scene, for instance, a sword is shoved up a soldier's rectum.

After the opening, Williams remarked that perhaps some theatre-goers had been genuinely shocked by some of the play's sentiments and language. But he wanted to assure everyone that Theatre Toronto was not preoccupied with vicarious presentations of horror, perversity, and savagery.

These things, he said, "are part of the reality of life, and the theatre exists to reveal truth and enrich us with understanding."

Well, perhaps. But I still don't think a sword up the rectum is part of the reality of life.

J osé Greco and His Spanish Dancers played the Royal
Alex numerous times. From the age of 24, the flam-
boyant flamenco artist had been an international
success.

One night after a show, José confided that he'd always
had to cope with "a terrible problem." He made it sound
like a terminal illness. When I asked what the problem
was, he said in a tone of bereavement, "My *dancers*. They
are forever leaving. I never drop anybody. They always
drop me."

I didn't have the nerve to ask why.

Due to the frequent defections, he said, he was
always forced to seek new talent. "I've found some fine
dancers in Arizona and New Mexico. In that part of the
States, they've retained a pure Spanish tradition—even
more than Mexico.

"But every year I go home to Spain and look for
young dancers in fiestas, ballet companies, clubs, and
dives. It's where I find some of my biggest stars."

"*And*," I noted, "some of the most extraordinarily
beautiful women."

José simply smiled. "I've been lucky. But I don't *look*
for beauty. I look for talent. For style. Personality. But . . .
if they happen to be beautiful as well," he winked, "then
I'm twice as lucky."

I asked why he made his women so prominent in a

*The multi-talented Sir Peter Ustinov can hold an audience
captive without props, costumes, or supporting players.
His one-man show was sold out when he played the
Royal Alex in 1996.*

traditionally male milieu.

"*You* should know that, Ed," José laughed. "In two words: 'Box office.'"

Sir Peter Ustinov has graced the stage of the Royal Alex on many occasions, most recently in 1996—a sold-out one-man show in which he simply sat on a stool and talked about his life.

Peter Ustinov could talk about cement and captivate an audience. Writer, actor, director, entertainer extraordinaire, he's one of the world's great raconteurs, incapable of cliché.

At a press conference before one show, someone mentioned director John Huston. "Ahhh, big, bad John," Ustinov said with a smile. Then he launched into an impromptu Huston anecdote that could have been an entire scene in a comedy.

"Huston is often naughty," Ustinov mused. "The man plays jokes on everyone. He got me on the set of *The African Queen* and caught me under one of those drenching machines. I was absolutely soaked and tiny Katharine Hepburn offered me her dry shirt." Peter patted his belly. "Can you *imagine?*

"But I had my revenge on John. They were behind schedule on *The African Queen*, and he came to see a play of mine in London, *The Love of Four Colonels*. I knew he was out front. So I got them to call him during intermission—from Charing Cross Hospital. Would he talk to Mr. Bogart? And of course they put him through on the phone to my dressing room."

Ustinov switches to a deep American voice. "This is John Huston here. Is Mr. Bogart there?"

Ustinov's voice is suddenly a whining Cockney. "I don't know. I'm the night man. I've only just come on. I've not been 'ere very long. I don't know this switchboard. Wojja say? Mister Boddice?"

Huston: "*Bogart!*"

Cockney: "You sure 'e's in 'ere?"

Huston: "Yes, I'm sure. I just got a message to call him."

Cockney: "Oh. Then 'e would be in 'ere, wouldn't 'e?"

Then, says Ustinov, "I started putting him through to various departments." He makes a buzzing phone sound.

An officious voice snaps: "I'll try to get you through."

A falsetto matron's voice: "Hellooo?"

Cockney: "Oh? Is this casualties?"

Matron: "No! This is maternity! I wish you wouldn't call me now."

Ustinov smiles through the roars of laughter. "I put Huston from one department to another, and he was in an absolutely desperate state. We finally got to casualties."

Huston: "Is Mr. Bogart there?"

A surgeon's slow ponderous voice: "Yes... This is Sir Henry Wills. I'm head of this casualty section. And I'm prevented by my Hippocratic oath from telling you what's wrong with Mr. Bogart. I'm waiting for a second, third and, indeed, fourth opinion, which should be here any hour now. But I can tell you, I don't think he'll be inactive for long. I don't think he'll be out of the film for more than three months."

Huston: "My Gawd... Do I understand... let me speak to him."

Surgeon: "No, sorry, I'm afraid you can't do that."

Ustinov is beaming. "John was almost choking. Eventually I relented because he sounded so unhappy. So I said:

Surgeon: "Well, I'll tell you what I think it is, anyway. Quite rare, quite a rare disease actually. It's a fractured eyelash. And, I'm afraid, a multiple fracture. It's fractured in two places. And it will mean him wearing a splint in his eyelash. We can avoid plaster because that makes blinking most difficult."

Ustinov stopped when the howls in the room

became too loud to hear him. Everyone applauded. I've seen standing ovations for far lesser performances.

One day someone asked Peter Ustinov what he thought of method acting. "A lot of the difficulty of celebrated method actors," he said, "was due to the fact that they were embarrassed to receive so much money for doing such a relatively easy job. They want to make it difficult.

"Olivier was working with a method actor once and gave him a direction. After a lot of grunting and much heavy thought, the actor asked what his motivation was. Exasperated, Olivier said, 'Your salary.'"

When Anne Murray opened in June 1978, she was the first solo musical star to appear on the Royal Alex's stage.

We, of course, were delighted to showcase the Maritime songbird who'd soared to international superstardom. And Anne was delighted because the Alex is her favourite theatre, one of the few she'll actually go to. Patrons who saw Katharine Hepburn in *A Matter of Gravity* and Maggie Smith in *Private Lives* did double-takes when they saw Ms. Murray sitting beside them.

Of the countless stars I've met through the years, Anne is one of the most unassuming.

She told me she'd just done the Merv Griffin show and bumped into Joey Bishop outside her dressing room. "Anne Murray!" said Bishop. "Why don't you ever say hello to me? Why don't you like me? We did a show 10 years ago, which you probably don't remember. And you wouldn't even speak to me then."

"Of course I remember," Anne told him. "It was with Glen Campbell in Hollywood. But you were such a big star I was too shy to say hello."

"That's crazy!" said Bishop. "You were the star of that show. You had the biggest hit record in the country."

"But," Anne protested, "I'd just got off the plane from Nova Scotia. I'd never even been to Hollywood before."

"Jeez," Joey said sheepishly. "All I knew was that you were the hottest thing in the music business. Everyone was playing 'Snowbird.' And you wouldn't even talk to me."

"Well, I'm sorry," said Anne, sticking out her hand. "Hello there, Joey."

She shook her head when she told me the story. "Can you believe it? Remembering that for all those years?"

Still, as Anne admitted, she'd never accepted stardom willingly. She'd shunned the Vegas Strip in the early seventies because, she said, "I don't particularly like being served up for dessert." But gradually she learned not to fight the acclaim.

"For years," she said, "I never thought of myself as being in show business. But I looked out the window of my hotel in Vegas and saw my name on the marquee at the Aladdin. Then I looked across the street at Caesar's Palace. And the marquee said Frank Sinatra. So I said to myself, 'Stop fighting it, kid. You're in the business.'"

Just months before appearing at the Alex, however, when asked to fill in for Bing Crosby at the O'Keefe Centre—reportedly at Crosby's fee—she said, "Sorry, but in August I'll be with my family in the Maritimes."

Yet even after accepting her celebrity status, Anne still maintained her irreverent Maritime wit, both publicly and in private. When her son, William Stewart Langstroth Jr., was born in 1976 (an event that rated number two on national newscasts; number one was Trudeau's cabinet shuffle), Anne woke to find her room flanked wall-to-wall with flowers. "I'm afraid to fold my hands on my chest," she murmured to her husband. "Someone might bury me."

During a performance in the States, she gleefully told me, an audience kept interrupting a song with standing ovations. "Finally, I hollered at them '*Ahhh, sidddddown!*' And they did."

She was also tickled about the time she introduced her song "Let's Keep It That Way," about marital infidelity. "I said, 'I'm sure everyone here's been unfaithful at one time or another.'

"It got no reaction, so I added, 'Or, at least, you *thought* about it.' And when *that* received no response, I looked out at all the Hollywood faces and said, 'Well, I'm sure you've all *read* about it.' And it brought the house down."

Which, when she played the Royal Alex, is exactly what Anne Murray did again.

I n 1975, just before Yul Brynner was due to open at the Alex in a new musical called *Odyssey*, we repainted all the backstage halls and dressing rooms. But before he arrived we received an extensive list of requests—including one that all halls and dressing room be painted a "dark brown."

And so we painted the backstage area again. I later

learned that Mr. Brynner had left a string of dressing rooms in theatres across the continent, from New York to California, all "dark brown."

Just before a matinée one Wednesday, Yul complained that his throat was sore, and he might not be able to go on. I paced the lobby, waiting for the wails inside when the announcement was made that his understudy would appear instead. Jokingly I said to the theatre manager, "If Telly Savalas was the understudy, I bet Brynner would go on."

A columnist for a Toronto paper overheard me. And the following day, my comment appeared in print. I was mortified—especially since Yul had gone on after all.

And it wasn't just mortification. I was also terrified that Yul would cancel the remainder of the run. So I sat down and wrote him a letter that read:

"Dear Mr. Brynner: My mother always said to me, 'Ed, you've got a big mouth. You always talk too much.' My mother was always right.

"So, Mr. Brynner, when I saw the article with my remark about you in the paper, I wanted to kill myself. I can only say that I owe you an apology, and hope you will accept it. It is a great honour to have you play our theatre. Sincerely, Ed Mirvish."

With the courage of a man facing execution, that night I went to his dressing room. Yul was sitting at his dressing table, but saw me in the mirror. For a minute there was silence, and I died inside.

Then he suddenly turned and smiled. "I got your letter, Ed," he said. "Don't kill yourself."

In 1978 we were proud to have Deborah Kerr as the star of *The Last of Mrs. Cheyney* at the Alex. It was a 50-year-old comedy by the now forgotten English playwright Frederick Lonsdale, a commoner who conned his way into the upper crust. In it, not surprisingly, Miss Kerr played a con artist who mixes with high society to aid her partner's second-storey operations.

Deborah said she was delighted to be playing comedy again, although she found it fatiguing. "In a drawing-room comedy of this style," she said, "when pace and timing are so important, your mind is racing a million miles a minute.

"If you take a pause in a drama or tragedy, if you take a little time to let the tears come up, it's fine. Here, if you take a pause, the whole thing drops like a bomb. It requires tremendous concentration. You're exhausted at the end of the day."

She was 57 at the time, a grandmother—but face

unlined, expression unruffled, she easily looked 15 years younger. Though she had an effortless, natural dignity, she had none of the airs of a "lady"—yet has always been considered proper. "And in some ways I am," she laughed. "I've always worn a bra. I'm not a bit 'with it.'"

Still, the high-class image was useful, she admitted, when in her mid-20s she first arrived in Hollywood. Unlike many American actresses who had to bear the crudity of studio moguls, Deborah was treated royally. "To prove they were really gentlemen," she recalled, "they bent over backwards to treat me well."

Yet by mid-career, Deborah decided they were treating her too well. Her roles were so tasteful she was finding them insipid. "It's because I was English, because of the accent. So they tended to treat me as prissy, with no sense of humour. I wasn't allowed to play a down-to-earth woman."

But then came the big break. With *From Here to Eternity*, Deborah Kerr graduated into red-blooded cinematic womanhood with a vengeance. In part she got the role through a fluke, Deborah said. She was under contract to MGM, which had cast her in a succession of costume pictures (*Quo Vadis, The Prisoner of Zenda, Young Bess*) with top billing but bloodless parts.

Meanwhile Harry Cohn, the tyrannical chief of Columbia Pictures, had acquired the rights to James

Jones's massive bestseller about U.S. soldiers in Hawaii just before Pearl Harbor, a book many considered too raw for the screen. But the early fifties was a period of testing movie censors, and Cohn (to his credit) ordered screenwriter Daniel Taradash to "get away with everything you can."

Cohn wanted screen vamp Joan Crawford to play the part of Karen Holmes, an officer's wife who was having affairs with enlisted men. Neither Taradash, producer Buddy Adler, nor director Fred Zinnemann wanted Crawford, but Harry Cohn insisted. Ironically, Crawford herself bowed out because she didn't like her costumes.

It was then that Deborah's agent, Bert Allenberg, called on Cohn to meekly suggest his client for the part. Cohn's response was immediate. "Why you stupid sonofabitch," he roared, "get out of here." Allenberg told Deborah he didn't think Cohn was too responsive to his suggestion.

That same afternoon, Zinnemann, Adler, and Taradash met Cohn in his office. "You know what that crazy sonofabitch Allenberg did?" Harry said. "He came in here and suggested Deborah Kerr for Karen."

The three men sat, then looked at each other, and suddenly they all said, "Of *course!*" Cohn couldn't believe what he was hearing. Finally Taradash convinced him that casting the Lady Deborah as a pseudo-tramp would "give the picture a new element of surprise."

And it did. Deborah's epochal love scene on a beach with Burt Lancaster became a film classic. After Karen Holmes, she never had to play Young Bess again.

Soon after *Eternity's* release, she got what she considered her most satisfying role: Laura in *Tea and Sympathy*. It was a part that permitted her to be both a "lady" and a woman with full emotional sensuality. She portrays a teacher's wife so moved by a schoolboy's fear of being homosexual that, at the play's climax, considered quite daring in the early fifties, she agrees to sleep with him.

"Bob Anderson did not know me when he wrote that part," she said, "but it was an extraordinary coming together of an actress and a role. Everything Laura was, I am. There's some part of you in every part you play, but generally a large part of you is left out. In *Tea and Sympathy* it was all there."

Acting, she said, is a career hopelessly dependent on luck. "It's like watching bullfights. You get one good one every two years."

Coming from her, it's a shocking statement. She's the last person in the world you'd consider an aficionado. But without losing a speck of poise, she explained that her husband, writer Peter Viertel (*White Hunter, Black Heart*), had written about bullfighting and was an intimate friend of the famous matador, Luis-Miguel Dominguin.

Then, as if she were playing with one's lingering image of her as the ultimate lady, she compared her own profession with Dominguin's. "Of all the jobs in the world, the one closest to being an actor is being a bullfighter. A 500-kilo bull is coming towards you like an express train—and you're not going to move your feet.

"That's what it's like to be an actor. Waiting for the curtain to go up is like the start of a bullfight, with the crowd, the music, and the pageantry. That's the only way to describe it.

"It's especially true in the theatre, where you have to go on knowing that everyone in the audience has read a review that went through you like an arrow. In movies it doesn't matter so much because by the time the film comes out you've mostly forgotten it—and you never have final control."

With bullfighting, she said, "I lost my whole ASPCA attitude when I saw a torero gored. People always say, 'Oh God, the poor bull,' and it's true the bull has no say in the matter, but they're bred to fight. You can't call it a sport. It's like show business, a mixture of art and business.

"But what raises it above that is that life and death are being played out before you. It's that thing of facing

*Above: Toronto theatre-goers have helped make Neil
Simon the most popular living playwright.
Pages following: Two of our popular Simon presentations.*

death, and facing it with courage, whether it's the man or the bull."

Besides her profound ability as an actress, I found Deborah Kerr an amazing woman.

Of the hundreds of road shows the Royal Alex has staged, Neil Simon has been our most prolific and successful supplier. I believe we've staged every Simon play that Broadway sent on the road, from *The Odd Couple*, *Plaza Suite*, and *Last of the Red Hot Lovers* to *The Sunshine Boys*, *The Gingerbread Lady*, *California Suite*, and *Prisoner of Second Avenue*.

Since the 1961 success of his first comedy, *Come Blow Your Horn*, he's become the most popular living playwright and has made more money than any dramatist in the history of theatre.

Hailed as "The King of Broadway Comedy," Simon not only had four plays running simultaneously on the Great White Way in 1967, but bought the Eugene O'Neill Theatre to stage new productions.

Not bad for a kid who co-wrote (with brother Danny) his first play at 15—staged by employees of a Brooklyn department store. "As a boy," he told me, "I

"You will laugh till the tears come."
Joel Siegel, WABC-TV

Ed and David Mirvish and The Citadel Theatre
in association with Ernest J. Schwarz & Brian Sewell present

Neil Simon's **Biloxi Blues**

Starring
Mitchell Whitfield

With
Louise Cranfield
Jennifer Dean
Mark Krause
Eric McCormack
John Ormerod
Cliff Saunders
Hugh Thompson

And
Leon Pownall
as Sgt. Toomey

Directed by
Brian Rintoul

Sets, props and lights designed by
Stancil Campbell

Costumes designed by
Shawn Kerwin

Co-sponsored by
TEN·TEN
CFRB
AM STEREO

THE TORONTO STAR

CHCH TV

Jan. 8-Feb. 20
593-4211

ROYAL ALEXANDRA

went to school. I listened to "The Shadow." I dreamt of being Joe Dimaggio. I went to the movies a lot and fell in love with Keaton, Laurel and Hardy, and Chaplin. I once got thrown out of a theatre for laughing too loudly at *Modern Times*. I was a nice, plain boy.

"When I read I'm America's most successful playwright, it amazes me. But I don't hold on to that for long, because I still often think of myself as that little boy growing up in the Bronx."

In the 1950s, Neil wrote gags for radio comics, then started supplying TV sketches to Sid Caesar, Garry Moore, and Phil Silvers. At 29, he was summoned to Hollywood to work on a Jerry Lewis special and took a two-month lease on a house.

The first week, he said, he gave Jerry two sketches. Lewis said they were fine for the show, and that was all he needed. Neil was dumbfounded. "But I've rented a house for seven more weeks," he said. "What do I do?"

Jerry shrugged. "Do whatever you want."

"And so," Neil said, "I went back to my rented house and started writing *Come Blow Your Horn*—though it took me three years to finish it." The show, of course, was an instant hit. And his next play, *Barefoot in the Park*, made his name.

"But would you believe," Neil confided, "in the original draft, *Barefoot* was set in a Swiss chalet? How does a play set in Switzerland eventually wind up in a little apartment off Third Avenue in Manhattan? Simple: I had a lot to learn.

"After many abortive attempts, I realized I had to take my *Barefoot* characters out of that exotic setting and stick closely to the truth, which was the reality of what happened in my first year of marriage."

Although initially known for his zinging one-liners, Neil admitted his approach had changed. "There's no joy anymore in repeating myself. I see humour in even the grimmest situations. So I think it's possible to write a play so moving, it can tear you apart and still have humour in it. I always try to find some human element.

"At first," he said, "all I ever wanted was to be the funniest writer in America, to write the funniest play. No longer. Creating laughter is relatively easy. And, I'll say with no modesty whatever, I have a lot of facility in this area.

"But laughs are not always a barometer. People can laugh their heads off and come out hating the play. But to make them laugh at the *right* things, ah, that's enormously fruitful. All I want is that the people who've just seen one of my plays will emerge from the theatre a little richer than when they went in. The laughter I like is the laughter that makes you jump, makes you aware."

I was thrilled when Myrna Loy appeared in Barefoot
in the Park *at the Royal Alex. I'd been a fan since
the* Thin Man *days.*

Since few Neil Simon plays have been flops, accusations that he's too prolific angered him. "If you want to talk about quantity, then Shakespeare has to be the biggest hack there ever was. If I can be as big a hack as Shakespeare, and as slick—terrific!"

Neil was also aware that he isn't popular with highbrow critics. "That's okay," he told me. "I've never intended to be highbrow. I'm happy to have my plays described as 'entertainments.'

"You have to be crazy to think of your plays as works of art. That would be like writing under the title, 'An important new play by Neil Simon.' That's pretentious. A work of art is qualitative. I haven't the slightest idea if what I'm writing is going to be a hit or a flop. It just feels good as I'm writing it."

Well, *I* know the difference between hits and flops. I've seen my share of both. But we've never had a flop from Mr. Simon. I only hope he "feels good" for a long time yet.

*B*arefoot in the Park, that huge Simon hit, played the Alex in 1969. Besides Richard Benjamin and Joan Van Ark, the comedy also starred the incred-

PETER O'TOOLE · ED MIRVISH · TONY BENNETT

Three boyos—Peter O'Toole, me, and Tony Bennett.

ible Myrna Loy, who I'd always loved as the dashing Thin Man's dazzling spouse.

One day at lunch I remarked on how much fun she must have had making those movies with William Powell. "You made a wonderful team," I told her.

Miss Loy thanked me and smiled demurely. "I hope you don't think I only teamed well with *Bill*," she said. "I also made some movies with a couple of other guys."

And, counting on her fingers, she ticked off the names of Ronald Colman, John Barrymore, Robert Montgomery, Spencer Tracy, Humphrey Bogart, Tyrone Power, Fredric March, and Rex Harrison.

She stopped and frowned. "Now who have I missed?" Myrna paused a moment, then beamed. "Oh yeah. There was also Cary Grant and Clark Gable."

That impetuous Irish boyo Peter O'Toole starred in two productions for us, *Uncle Vanya* and *Present Laughter*, which played in tandem at the Alex.

Though, at 30, he sprang to instant stardom as *Lawrence of Arabia*'s preening persona, Peter had already spent nearly a decade honing his craft on stage. Gaining a scholarship to the Royal Academy of Dramatic Arts, he studied two years with such other unknowns as Alan Bates and Brian Bedford—plus another pair who subsequently matched his rollicking reputation, Albert Finney and Richard Harris.

It was, O'Toole told me, "the most remarkable class the academy ever had. Although at the time, we weren't reckoned for much. They considered us all completely dotty."

In 1955, Peter joined the Bristol Old Vic and, in the following 42 months, played a total of 73 roles. Beginning as a cabby in *The Matchmaker*, he went on to such diverse roles as the Duke of Cornwall in *King Lear*, Peter Shirley in *Major Barbara*, Mr. Jaggers in *Great Expectations*, Alfred Doolittle (if you can imagine it) in *Pygmalion*, and Jimmy Porter in *Look Back in Anger*.

It's an amazing demonstration of O'Toole's skill in interpreting character roles. But, as Peter pointed out, "Acting is, by definition, character acting. The French make a distinction between an *acteur* and a *comedien*. An *acteur* takes a recurring role. A *comedien* can take on any role. I prefer to consider myself a *comedien*."

But then, as though embarrassed, Peter tossed back his head and snorted, "Oh Lord, I'm really loath to discuss myself in such ponderous terms. Basically, what I am is a *jobbing* actor. Acting's what my *job* is. Have jockstrap, will travel."

Then he laughs. "You see, the only person I have to satisfy is *me*, since I see myself as the author's advocate. I think acting is making words flesh." Long pause. "Though, I admit, I've never achieved total satisfaction.

"But I'm also a performer, an entertainer. And I do love theatre, perhaps more than anything. You make a lot of pals, meeting each other for brief intervals, under all sorts of tension, working together for a while, then separating. It's a thrilling existence."

That wonderful lady and actress Joan Plowright played the Alex in 1991, along with her son and daughter, in *Time and the Conways*. But her late husband, Sir Laurence Olivier—who was artistic director of London's Old Vic before I bought it—still played a major part in most of our conversations.

Joan had us in stitches one night when she showed how Lord Olivier always milked his curtain calls. "Larry always said there was nothing more exhilarating than hanging onto a curtain and letting the audience know that you'd sweated blood, given your all in the definitive performance—just for *them*."

Then, with perfect mimicry, she described how superbly staged his curtain calls were:

First, his eyes take in the gallery and hold for a moment. Then his eyes take in the upper circle, and hold another moment. Then he would eye the dress circle—and hold longer, for there's more money there. Then he'd eye the stalls for even longer. And finally his eyes would go from left to right on the boxes, with a reverence accorded royalty.

Then, he would let his head sink slowly down till his

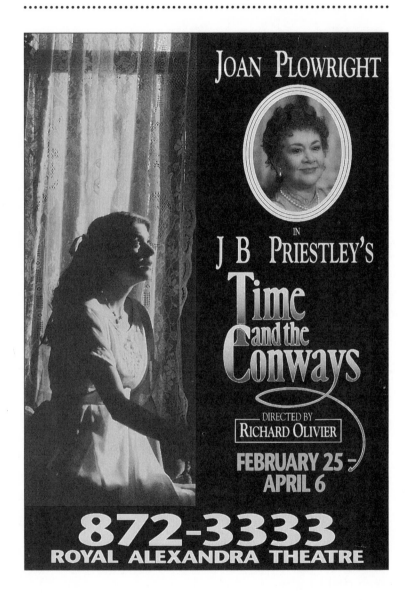

JOAN PLOWRIGHT

IN

J B PRIESTLEY'S

Time and the Conways

DIRECTED BY
RICHARD OLIVIER

FEBRUARY 25 –
APRIL 6

872-3333
ROYAL ALEXANDRA THEATRE

chin met his chest, exuding modesty to the hilt. The applause would swell. At last the head would come up, his eyes wide and glittering. And everyone knew he was thinking, "Is this really for me? It can't be for me. I can't believe it. What have I done to deserve such applause? I am only a mere player, your humble servant."

He would wait a minute, reeking humility, then throw his outstretched arms to the company on either side. For after all, dear audience, without the company, my splendid fellow players, I would be nothing. He would wait a long beat, then move forward. And then, with hand on heart, he would take his slow final bow.

Sometimes he'd step forward and say, "My dear friends, thank you. I would stay with you longer, but I am completely exhausted and must go." By then, of course, the entire audience was erupting in a standing ovation.

Joan Plowright laughed. "As Larry always said, 'If they're not on their feet by that time, you've done something terribly wrong.'"

Joan Plowright starred in Time and the Conways. *It was a family affair as evidenced by this poster. Richard Olivier, the director, is her son.*

In 1993 we played Willy Russell's musical *Blood Brothers* at the Alex, and Willy came from Liverpool for the opening.

He said it was the culmination of a dream. He'd always wanted to write a musical—and not just the book and lyrics, but the music as well. "People said I was absolutely daft. The book? Well, yes. The lyrics? Possibly. But the music? Never! And I could well understand their objections.

"At school," Willy chuckled, "a succession of my music teachers reported that I showed no talent. One even said that if I continued my music course, he'd be tempted to tender his resignation. The same man said he'd consider it an achievement, 'if Willy even learned to play the gramophone.'"

But when writing the play, Russell told me, he had constant nightmares of a million critical reviews, night-

Michael Burgess and Amy Sky, two Canadians, starred in Blood Brothers. *Michael had already been a hit in* Les Misérables, *but this was Amy's first performance in an acting role on the Toronto stage.*

*Above: David Cassidy and Mark Hutchinson in the pose
that was used on the cover of the program for*
Blood Brothers, *right.*

mares that woke him soaked in sweat. One in particular
said, "It is plain that the composer doesn't know a
crotchet from a hatchet, though I would readily concede
that armed with a hatchet Mr. Russell could do no worse
damage than he could with a crotchet."

Fortunately, when *Blood Brothers* opened, the reviews
were kinder than those in his dreams. Still, he didn't lack
critical attacks.

"I was driving to Wales with my family," Willy said,

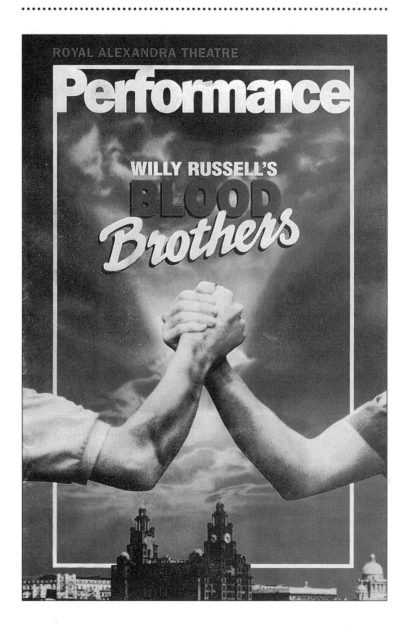

"when a song from *Blood Brothers* came on the radio. I was reaching over to turn up the volume when a small voice in the back seat piped up, 'Oh *no*, not that bloody song again.'

"I turned and scowled, '*Ruthie*, don't swear.' But still, fair is fair. I slipped in a cassette of her favourite nursery rhymes, and we sang 'Lavender's Blue' and 'Cock-A-Doodle-Do' all the way to Wales."

One of the greatest hits in the Royal Alex's history was Michael Bennett's long-running musical, *A Chorus Line*.

When it opened in Toronto, the show had won every top award, revitalized Broadway, and (because of the money it made) spurred a sudden resurgence of musicals. It also, almost overnight, made Michael Bennett famous and a multimillionaire.

But just four years before the show's smash Broadway debut, Michael told me, he'd harboured thoughts of "moving to New Zealand and starting a stock company with revivals of *South Pacific* for the good people of Christchurch."

It wasn't that he hadn't experienced success. He'd

already choreographed such Broadway hits as *Company*, *Follies*, and *Promises, Promises*, and directed Katharine Hepburn in *Coco*. He'd also been nominated for a slew of Tonies, but never got one. "I went to the Tony ceremonies six years in a row without winning a thing," he said. "It was like going to a birthday party year after year and never getting any cake.

"A lot of my work was overlooked or miscredited. Some of the best work I ever did was on *Company*. Hal Prince called me his co-director, yet my billing read something like 'Musical Sequences Directed By.' The play won every award that year except for choreography."

Michael blamed the situation largely on the press for its indifference. What kept him from charging off to Christchurch, he said, was the experimental show he was working on, *A Chorus Line*. Rather than having a conventional book written, Michael had hired several writers to re-work the tape-recorded autobiographies of a group of "gypsies"—the term for chorus-line dancers who go from musical to musical.

One of the gypsies, whom Bennett later married, was Donna McKechnie, who'd always had the problem (which the show eventually highlighted) of being too good a dancer to blend into a chorus line. Another of the gypsies was Bennett himself, whose Broadway career began in 1961 as a dancer in *Subways Are for Sleeping*.

One of the most-quoted lines from that show was Michael's own, when he said, "I realized committing suicide in Buffalo was redundant." It hardly made him a hero in his own home town—and he didn't consider it entirely a coincidence that, on the same day he won a Pulitzer Prize for *Chorus Line*, the Buffalo cops arrested his dad on nine bookmaking charges.

Bennett rehearsed his fledgling show on a stage of Joseph Papp's Shakespeare Festival Public Theatre in a "workshop" situation—meaning performers were paid very little but would get a percentage of any profit. He said he later learned that the Shubert Organization (which was largely responsible for reinvigorating New York theatre at the time) had been giving Papp money to continue the project.

It was common knowledge that Papp himself had mixed emotions about the show, and even wanted to close it just prior to its opening. Ironically, Papp's Shakespeare Festival was later heavily subsidized by *Chorus Line*'s massive profits.

Though the Shuberts provided funds to keep the project alive, the amount was limited. Instead of the $120,000 Bennett wanted for the show's grand finale (which, with lavish costumes and gala entrances would have "starred" the lucky gypsies chosen for the chorus line), he got only $60,000.

In retrospect, Bennett said, it was probably for the best. He was able to afford the glossy costumes for his dancers' closing number with the famous mirrored wall behind them, but instead of highlighting individual stars, the entire chorus line appeared.

"But," Michael laughed, "the main thing was that my mother loved the final ending. It implied that *all* the gypsies got jobs."

In 1984 I was given the title "Freeman of the City of London," making me a member of an old and honourable company. This award was given to me for our work in theatre, as well as for restoring the historic Old Vic, which had been built in 1818.

I mention this award not to brag, but because of its two unique advantages. As a Freeman of the City of London, I instantly had the following privileges: I am allowed to take my sheep across London Bridge without paying a toll tax. Also, if I'm ever condemned to be hanged for a crime, they must hang me with a silken rope, not hemp.

And to think if I wasn't in show business, I'd never be able to enjoy these side benefits whenever I visit England.

Whitehead-Stevens, George W. George
and Frank Milton
present
The National Theatre
of Great Britain Company in
a new comedy

Bedroom Farce

by
Alan Ayckbourn

Designed by
Timothy O'Brien & Tazeena Firth
Lighting by
Peter Radmore
Sets & Lighting Supervised by
Marc B. Weiss
Directed by
Alan Ayckbourn and Peter Hall

Bedroom Farce *by Alan Ayckbourn was a big hit with our audiences in 1979. This poster is the one done for the National Theatre's presentation the previous year.*

One of the most hilarious comedies to play the Royal Alex was Alan Ayckbourn's *Bedroom Farce* in 1979.

When it had opened in London the year before, the leading critic, Bernard Levin, called it "a perfect comedy, in which we had nothing to do but laugh." Another critic invited his readers to sue him if they didn't laugh till their sides split.

I only wish all our comedies would get such reviews. But they're typical with almost all of Ayckbourn's plays. For as one of Britain's most prolific and popular playwrights (often with two plays running simultaneously in London's West End), Alan is to England what Neil Simon is to the States.

Ironically, they share something else in common. Simon's comedies are always more successful in Toronto than in London, while Ayckbourn's work transfers better to the Royal Alex than to Broadway. It must say something for Canadian audiences.

But certainly *Bedroom Farce* proved as big a hit at the Alex as in London. The comedy unfolds in three bedrooms in three different houses, but all featured in a single stage-set. "I made it three bedrooms," Alan said, "because I like threes. It's a comic number. Besides, back home, in Scarborough's Theatre in the Round, where all my plays first open, I couldn't get more beds on the stage."

He told me *Bedroom Farce* had been specially commissioned by the National Theatre, "so I was finally forced to write it during three or four sleepless nights." Unlike Neil Simon, who said he loved writing, Ayckbourn maintained he hated it. "It's why I try to get it over with as quickly as possible. For 360 days a year I *think* about writing, contemplate and consider writing, and successfully avoid it."

He said as a playwright he had three desires. "To write what I dream I'm going to write and not what I actually write. To like a play of mine five years after I've written it. And not to have my plays included in any school syllabus and find out what it's like to be loathed by an entire generation of schoolkids."

We all make humiliating gaffes in life. Alan Ayckbourn said one of his most embarrassing moments was mailing two letters in the wrong envelopes. The first letter was intended for two film producers who had "dined and wined me endlessly and pointlessly" the previous night. But it went to his mystified agent instead.

The second letter to his agent, describing in detail the dreadful ordeal he'd just gone through, went to the producers.

Ten years later Ayckbourn found himself dining with the same two men and had to inform them that they wouldn't get a film from him and never would. "In the ensuing silence," Alan said, "one of them began to tell the story about the young writer he'd once met, 'who put the wrong letter in the wrong...'

"At this point our eyes met in mutual recognition. 'Do go on,' I pleaded, but he refused."

John Gielgud also recalled his "moment of extreme mortification," when Clement Attlee was prime minister of England. Gielgud said he'd been asked to join Attlee for supper at the Falcon Hotel, following a performance at Stratford-upon-Avon. At the table Gielgud was seated beside a young lady he'd never met, and the conversation turned to where they lived.

Sir John Gielgud and Richard Baker on the Lilian Baylis Terrace at the National Theatre in 1983. Both actors have appeared at the Old Vic and the Royal Alex.

"I told her I had a very convenient home in Westminster," Gielgud said, "an easy to walk to the theatre. Then I asked, 'And where do you live?'

"She looked distinctly surprised, and replied somewhat curtly, 'Number ten, Downing Street.'

"No one had told me she was Attlee's daughter. I could only reply, 'How nice.'"

Robert Morley told me the story about playwright Tom Stoppard's memorable gaffe at the time his play *Travesties* was running in London. Stoppard was called one afternoon by his friend, John Wells, to say he was going to the play that night with the man who was to translate *Travesties* into French. Wells asked Stoppard to meet them in the manager's office during intermission.

Sure enough, at the end of Act 1, Wells arrived at the office followed by a long-haired young man who shook Stoppard's hand and announced, "I loff your text."

Then, when Wells went off to the loo, Stoppard concentrated on the stranger in his dashing French suit who, he thought, somewhat resembled Rudolf Nureyev. The man apologized about not being able to understand the play completely at one viewing, but said he looked forward to reading it.

Stoppard then backed him into a corner and gave him a five-minute rundown on some of the difficulties he could expect to encounter. The man looked baffled as Stoppard babbled on about the changes he still planned to make, promising to send him a copy as soon as he'd finished.

By the time Wells returned, the man was looking haunted, but Stoppard was still rambling on.

"What are you *doing*, Tom?" Wells asked with alarm.

"I'm giving him suggestions," Stoppard said, "about the play's translation."

"Oh for God's sake, he's not the French translator," Wells snorted, as another man, smoking a Gauloise, entered the office. "That's Rudolf Nureyev."

Robert Morley's own great gaffe occurred at a luncheon party, when he found himself chatting to a distinguished-looking chap from Canberra, and said, "I do envy you living in Australia. So few of we British have the sense to cut and run."

Then, Morley told me, "Realizing that my opening phrase might suggest some sort of criminal activity, I enquired as to his occupation, thus letting him know I was fully aware he was not an absconding banker."

The man gave Morley a long, piercing look and replied, "I'm the governor general, and we've already been introduced twice over cocktails."

Morley also told a story about shooting the movie *Beat the Devil* in Ravello. The producer David O. Selznick was also on location because his wife, Jennifer Jones, was the female lead. "Although it wasn't one of his own pictures," Morley said, "the great interferer, as we called him, had decided Jennifer's wardrobe must outdo those of her fellow star, Gina Lollobrigida.

"So Selznick had summoned the great couturier, Monsieur Givenchy, from Paris to deck her out. Givenchy arrived breathless and exhausted, but bearing sets of hastily stitched toiles. Not the dresses, mind you, but the simple cotton patterns.

"Selznick was enraptured. 'Ah, how clever of you, Monsieur,' he burbled, 'to dress my wife entirely in white.'

"The astonished Givenchy wisely took the money and instantly flew home."

Bing Crosby called him "the greatest singer I've ever heard." Frank Sinatra called him "the best in the business. He's the singer who gets across what composers had in mind—probably a little more."

*The classy Tony Bennett. His newfound popularity is
well deserved and is an indication of the timeless
quality of his work.*

Both "the Crooner" and "the Voice" were referring, of
course, to "the Singer's Singer," Tony Bennett. He played
in concert to packed houses at the Alex in 1978, and I'm
proud to say we've been friends ever since.

He's an artist, of course, not only on stage but in oils.
At one of Tony's first art shows, I purchased one of his
early paintings, a lovely landscape of Italy's Amalfi Drive.
It hangs in our restaurant next door to the theatre, so our
patrons can enjoy it as much as I do. It is signed, as all
his paintings are, with the name he was christened with
in 1926: Anthony Dominick Benedetto.

Today, although he's about the last of his amazing generation, Bennett's probably an even bigger star than at any time during his long career. But, as Sinatra said, he's the best. And Frank should know. Tony's career was just beginning in the early 1950s, at a time when Frank's was foundering.

Born in Astoria, Long Island, Tony studied both music and painting in his teens. He worked in his uncle's grocery (a business I also grew up in), was a singing waiter in a local restaurant, and finally worked his way up to elevator operator at the Park Sheraton hotel. Near the end of World War II he did some mopping up with the army in Germany and France.

Yet his warmest memories are of the era in which he started singing. "I ought to be envied," he's told me, "because I grew up during a great time for music. In fact, one of my voice teachers, Miriam Spier, lived right on 52nd Street when it was alive with all the immortal jazz artists in those little clubs.

"She told me, 'Just listening to them will be your best lesson.' And, of course, it was. Because there were all those giants like Joe Williams, Stan Getz, Billie Holiday, Erroll Garner, Lester Young, Art Tatum, George Shearing—all working within one block on this street, all marvellous inspirations.

"There was so much healthy competition, so much

love exchanged. Whereas today, it's almost a feeling of 'Let's put the music through computers. Let's not get emotionally involved.'"

When talking of song interpreters, of which Tony himself is considered the finest, he says, "Nowadays they are minimized. In fact, the interpreter very often is the writer himself. When Arlen or Berlin or Porter composed a tune, you could do it as a march, as a ballad, as a waltz, or in straight 4/4. There was something special about the craft of writing a great song.

"Since then—well, take someone like Paul Williams, for instance, who's written terrific songs. But the problem is, they're one-dimensional. Songs like his are good for the guy who writes and performs them, but there isn't much that can be done with them. They don't filter down to the instrumental soloists and become permanent jazz standards like so many of the forties and fifties songs."

Tony's sincere concern for excellence, he says, was a constant source of friction between him and Columbia records, the label he stuck with for 24 years after his first hit single in 1950, "Boulevard of Broken Dreams." He recorded 580 songs for the company, including 74 albums, but says it was always a battle. "I had to fight for the material I wanted, until it became too nerve-racking."

Leaving Columbia, Tony set up his own company, Improv Records, in partnership with the owner of

Buffalo's Statler Hilton hotel. "It was one of the smartest things I ever did," he told me. "I saw too many of my contemporaries buckling under, singing songs deliberately aimed at a young listening audience. And, in most cases, these ploys failed. Because kids want to hear songs performed by someone their own age."

Still, Tony says, "I think there's a whole army of fans who want a certain kind of music and find it isn't being produced any more. Today, too many producers completely ignore the basic melodic values. Meanwhile, people who like their music without gimmicks pour through the bins and say, 'Gee, I never got this one.' So they buy it." Tony grins. "And I get these big royalty cheques."

One thing he's always loved is working with jazzmen. Over the years he's done numerous tours with big bands such as Duke Ellington's and Woody Herman's, and recorded an album with Count Basie's orchestra. "I trust my own judgement," he says. "That's why I use great musicians, and the reason I stick to quality songs instead of going with the nine-day wonders.

"When you think back to all the giants—Sinatra, Dorsey, and all the instrumentalists and band leaders who made a lasting mark on musical history—how did they do it? They just listened to the public and gave them the best they could offer.

"It's why the TV specials in Britain are more musically authentic than ours. In the States, they take a marvellous singer like Ray Charles and give him just one or two numbers in an hour-long show. In England, they give him a whole 60-minute special of his own.

"Lena Horne's done TV specials in England unlike anything she's ever had the chance to do at home. Bing Crosby found the same freedom of expression in London, where he made his last two albums—one on his own and one with Fred Astaire. It all boils down to the simple premise of assuming people do want the best entertainment."

It was in England that Tony made the TV appearance of which he is proudest. "I had the privilege of celebrating the hundredth anniversary of the Royal Albert Hall with the London Philharmonic. It was the first time I'd sung with a symphony orchestra, and Lord, what a fantastic experience.

"Laurence Olivier inspired me. He said he never played for himself, but just for the audience. He considered himself an entertainer who simply wanted to please people. That's always been my philosophy, and my career has been just beautiful because of it. And in return, the public trusts me.

"I think the majority of people are smarter than people give them credit for. How come Woody Allen movies find their way to the top? How come Vladimir Horowitz sells so many records? It's one of the most wonderful things that can happen in this commercialized business."

The big question, of course, is if Bing and Frank considered Tony the best, what singers does *he* most admire? Without pausing, he says, "Joe Williams, of course. And Frank Sinatra, for everything he's done. Ella, Sarah, Peggy Lee and, of course, Lena. She's the most disciplined singer I have ever heard, male or female."

At another time, he said, "I'm like Duke Ellington, in that I deplore the use of categories. Art knows no boundaries. A primitively painted church window in Harlem has the same value as a stained glass window in Rome. You never know where the next great artistic stimulus will come from.

"You know what Sinatra told me many years ago? He said, 'Money follows talent. Create the talent and someone will want it.' So I'm firmly convinced that despite all the problems young people face today, the best is yet to come."

Maybe so. But *I'm* still convinced that with Tony Bennett we've got the best already.

ndré-Philippe Gagnon started early as a comic impressionist. As a bashful kid in the Quebec City suburb of Loretteville, he was doing impersonations of the cartoon canary Tweetie Bird at five. "The main thing," he recalls, "was to make my friends laugh. Even then it was the dream I had." Today, through his stage and TV shows, Gagnon's making millions roar with laughter.

Whether he's aping the stars of the Simpson trial (including both Katos, house guest and dog) in his wickedly witty number, "O.J.: The Musical"; satirizing the Royal Family's sexual travails; or mimicking Bill Clinton's famed *Tonight Show* saxophone jazz riff (which Gagnon does on a microphone), his imitations are both dead-on and deadly.

In a show uniquely combining superb stand-up comedy and concert, the blond, boyish Gagnon (who charms audiences within seconds of striding on stage) switches in microseconds from Mick Jagger to Satchmo, from Durante to Sting (using barrel-voiced James Earl Jones and a bafflegabbing Jean Chrétien as emcees), and can start a song in Joe Cocker's gravelly croon and end it as Dionne Warwick.

If there's one voice Gagnon recreates effortlessly, it's that of his idol, Frank Sinatra. "I'm never scared when I do Sinatra," he told me. "It's a sound that comes easily to me."

When he first brought his show to the Alex in 1996 (breaking a four-week box-office record), he gave at least 130 rapid-fire impressions from the 300 voices in his repertoire—not including his virtuoso rendering of all 18 voices in the legendary famine relief number, "We Are the World," which has become Gagnon's classic.

Starting off in small Quebec clubs, it was André-Philippe's appearance at Montreal's Just for Laughs comedy festival in 1985, followed by a gig on Johnny Carson's *Tonight Show* that launched his career as one of Canada's top comics—in both French and English.

After headlining a show in Switzerland with Sinatra and Jane Fonda, his first Quebec tour sold 525,000 tickets, and two million Quebecers saw his first TV special. Soon he was breaking house records from Brisbane, Brussels, and Vancouver to Las Vegas. He played the prestigious Casino de Paris and the Grand Prix de Monaco, and sold out the Royal Alex again in 1997.

Gagnon says while his 250 shows a year are physically taxing, he has to keep touring to sell himself. "Unlike Celine Dion or Roch Voisine, there are no CDs working for me. Today it's all a mad rush. My family has to make a lot of sacrifices." Which is why he still rushes home between shows, as he did from the Alex each week, to his wife and baby daughter in Quebec.

Yet even with his stunning success, Gagnon says he's still afraid of disappointing his audiences. "So every night," he told me, "I try to add nuances that will improve my comedy, my acting, my dancing. I try to be as sharp as possible. That's why I tell myself that each show I'm performing is a première."

Gagnon need hardly worry about disappointing audiences. They even laugh through the intermissions.

When we bought the Royal Alex, I found filing cabinets and boxes filled with playbills, photographs, and news clippings dating back through the decades, bearing such names as Joe E. Brown, John, Lionel and Ethel Barrymore, Orson Welles, Al Jolson, Paul Robeson, Edith Evans, Tallulah Bankhead, Fred and Adele Astaire, Gertrude Lawrence, Ethel Waters, Bette Davis, Humphrey Bogart, Sidney Greenstreet, Edward G. Robinson, Tyrone Power, Maurice Chevalier, C. Aubrey Smith, Alfred Lunt, and Lynn Fontaine—all had trod the theatre's boards.

Among the memorabilia was a yellowed review of the 1924 presentation of Sophocles' *Oedipus Rex* starring Sir John Martin-Harvey. The *Telegram's* smitten critic was moved to call the production "class of the first water, the finest tragedy Toronto has ever seen."

He went on to rave about "the background, altars glowing with incense-breathing braziers, the bronze-bossed doors, the massive columns, the marble steps of many-gated Thebes; the action, continuous for two hours; the acting, in a word, perfect."

Boy! Over the years, I could certainly have used *that* guy.

Following pages: A very small selection of the playbills I inherited with the wonderful theatre building. The one from 1917 must have been folded and stuck in a patron's pocket or purse as it's rather crumpled and folded, but I like that—I feel as if it could have been clasped in someone's hands just yesterday. By the 1920s, the programs, which were printed in two colours, carried advertising on the covers; inside were more advertisements, for Welsh coal; cravats "reasonably priced" from $2 to $5; a Dodge sedan for $1,535; and just to prove that some things have gone down in price, radios for $230. In the 1930s and through to the 1950s, the programs were printed in black and white and the advertising had moved to only the inside pages. The two undated playbills were likely from the thirties—look at those names: Alfred Lunt, Lynn Fontaine, and Myrna Loy in an early appearance.

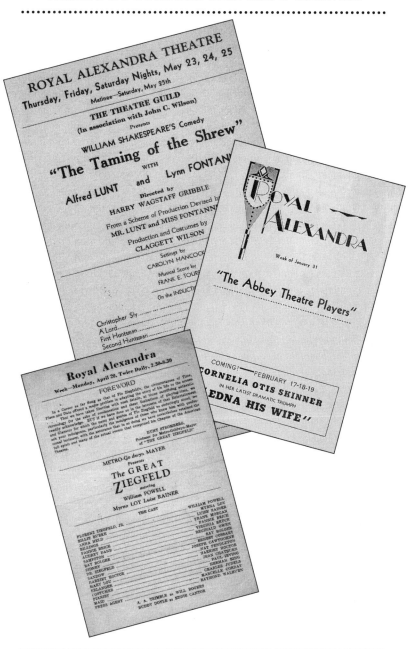

ROYAL ALEXANDRA THEATRE
Thursday, Friday, Saturday Nights, May 23, 24, 25
Matinee—Saturday, May 25th

THE THEATRE GUILD
(In association with John C. Wilson)
Presents

WILLIAM SHAKESPEARE'S Comedy

"The Taming of the Shrew"
WITH
Alfred LUNT and Lynn FONTAN

Directed by
HARRY WAGSTAFF GRIBBLE
From a Scheme of Production Devised b
MR. LUNT and MISS FONTANN
Production and Costumes by
CLAGGETT WILSON

Settings by
CAROLYN HANCOC

Musical Score by
FRANK E. TOUR

(In the INDUCTI

Christopher Sly
A Lord
First Huntsman
Second Huntsman

ROYAL
ALEXANDRA

Week of January 31

"The Abbey Theatre Players"

COMING!——FEBRUARY 17-18-19
CORNELIA OTIS SKINNER
IN HER LATEST DRAMATIC TRIUMPH
"EDNA HIS WIFE"

Royal Alexandra
Week—Monday, April 20, Twice Daily, 2.30-8.30

FOREWORD
In a Career as far flung as that of Flo Ziegfeld, the circumstances of Time,
Place and Date offered a major problem in adapting the story of his life to the screen.
That we have taken liberties with such details as times, sequence of playing authentic
incidents, for the sake of continuation and sheer fundament of that Entertainment, we
readily acknowledge. BUT if we have done so in the moments of that Entertainment, we
and Glamour for which the name have spoken of those who knew him with profes-
sek your indulgence, with the assurance that in so doing you have nevertheless retained the
full spirit and many of the actual events that composed his life.
Theatre.

BUNT STROMBERG,
Producer for Metro-Goldwyn-Mayer
of "THE GREAT ZIEGFELD"

METRO-Goldwyn MAYER
Presents

The GREAT
ZIEGFELD
starring
William POWELL
Myrna LOY Luise RAINER

THE CAST
WILLIAM POWELL
MYRNA LOY
LUISE RAINER
FRANK MORGAN
FANNIE BRICE
VIRGINIA BRUCE
REGINALD OWEN
RAY BOLGER
FLORENZ ZIEGFELD, JR.
BILLIE BURKE
ANNA HELD
BILLINGS
FANNIE BRICE
AUDREY DANE
SAMPSTON
SIDNEY
RAY BOLGER
DR. ZIEGFELD
SANDOW
HARRIET HOCTOR
MARY LOU
ERLANGER
COSTUMER
PIANIST
MAID
PRESS AGENT
ERNEST COSSART
JOSEPH CAWTHORNE
NAT PENDLETON
HARRIET HOCTOR
JEAN CHATBURN
PAUL IRVING
HERMAN BING
CHARLES JUDELS
MARCELLE CORDAY
RAYMOND WALBURN
A. A. TRIMBLE as WILL ROGERS
BUDDY DOYLE as EDDIE CANTOR

He concluded his panting review with the words, "What could possibly follow Oedipus?"

Out of sheer curiosity, I checked the old bookings to find out what *did* come next to the Royal Alex's stage. Well, how about Groucho, Harpo, Chico, and Zeppo?

The Marx Brothers had brought their musical comedy in for a sell-out week. I looked, but couldn't find, a review by the *Tely* pundit—if indeed the breathless tragedy-buff even wrote one. According to the other critics, the boys were hilarious.

I also picked up a bit of trivia. In their early days on stage, Harpo wore a bright scarlet wig, which in black and white pictures looks brown. When the brothers began making movies, he switched his wig to blond.

In 1967 we celebrated the Royal Alexandra's Diamond Jubilee. Four weeks before, I told my wife, "Go ahead and organize something special, Anne." And boy, did she ever. As the *Toronto Telegram* raved, "It was better than Confederation."

Prior to the show, we threw a cocktail party at the Royal York Hotel. As we'd suggested in our invitations, most guests arrived wearing period costumes, from top hats to hoopskirts. Afterwards, everyone rode the few blocks to the theatre in ancient landaus and antique cars. A contingent of police lined the route as crowds on the sidewalks cheered the Model Ts and old hansom carriages with their gaily garbed passengers.

At the theatre, they were helped down from their carriages by a costumed, bewhiskered doorman, then they entered on a long red carpet that stretched beneath the Royal Alex's marquee. Inside, each gentleman received a Jubilee Rose boutonnière, while the ladies were all given a "diamond" souvenir—of which five were real diamonds.

Before the show, a telegram sent from London by Ralph Richardson was read. It said, "The Royal Alexandra is a precious ornament of Toronto and it is fitting that it should receive a diamond." Sir Ralph also recalled that he'd once refused to appear in any Toronto productions unless they were staged in "the great King Street shrine."

The performance that night was the dazzling première of the Royal Winnipeg Ballet—in which, like a true-to-life Hollywood cliché, Swedish ballerina Annette Wiedersheim stepped in at the very last moment to dance the leading role in *Aimez-Vous Bach*, which had been choreographed by her famous husband, Brian Macdonald. During the wave of curtain calls, Annette and the dancers got thunderous applause.

The audience was filled with celebrities. From the theatre world were entertainers Barbara Chilcott, Bruno Gerussi, Amelia Hall, Jan Rubes, Sean Mulcahy, Robert Christie, Dave Broadfoot, Ed McGibbon, and Sandra O'Neill.

Canada's theatre establishment was represented by The New Play Society's Dora Mavor Moore, the National Ballet's Celia Franca, the St. Lawrence Centre's Mavor Moore, the National Arts Centre's G. Hamilton Southam, the Stratford Festival's Floyd Chalmers and Tom Patterson, Spring Thaw's Robert Johnson, the Dominion Drama Festival's Laurier Melanson, the National Theatre School's Mrs. Donald McGibbon, and the Actor Fund of Canada's Jane Mallett.

From Montreal's Expo 67, which was capturing the world's attention that year, came John Pratt. The CBC was represented by Norman Campbell, Leo Orenstein, Robert Hall, and Adrienne Clarkson. And a surprise guest was Earle Grey, who'd formerly run Toronto's Shakespeare Festival, and had just returned from England. Politicians included past and present Toronto mayors and Ontario lieutenant-governors.

Afterwards, the crinolines and tail-coats all swept next door to Ed's Warehouse where wine flowed freely at an elegant roast beef buffet. The party was joined by TV's Art Linkletter, the great band leader Percy Faith, and

Lorne Greene who, while riding to fame in "Bonanza," was still part of Toronto's theatre establishment.

It was a wonderful night, a wonderful show, a wonderful bash. As the *Telegram* summed it up, "There'll never be another party like this, ever."

The 1967 season also included such diverse shows as Hal Holbrook's brilliant one-man show *Mark Twain Tonight*, a South African revue entitled *Wait A Minim*, Helen Hayes in *The Show Off*, the New York City Center's *Joffrey Ballet* and *The Bristol Old Vic*.

But by far our biggest hit that year was the Charlottetown Festival's smash musical, *Anne of Green Gables*, which has since, of course, become a Canadian classic. It broke every Royal Alex box-office record.

The *Toronto Star's* Sid Adelman pointed out that in the Royal Alex's 60-year history, only four shows had completely sold out before they opened. And three of them were Canadian—*Anne of Green Gables*, *Tit-Coq* and *My Fur Lady*. The fourth was Olsen and Johnston's *Hellzapoppin*.

The *Merce Cunningham Dance Company* filled the Royal Alex's stage in 1978. The group, through the years, had been both revered (as original) and reviled (as robotic.) But by the time its dancers flew into Toronto (with tons of freight), Cunningham's company was considered an American institution.

In the fifties and sixties, Merce told me, they made annual college tours across the States, hoping to build a potential audience. And the entire company, including props, costumes, and sound equipment, travelled en masse in a Volkswagen bus, usually with Merce at the wheel.

It wasn't until a barnstorming six-month world tour in 1964, he said, that critics in Europe, especially Britain, recognized him for bringing dance abreast of contemporary art and music. After that, in New York (where his company was based) the critics suddenly took Cunningham seriously, calling him one of the "establishment" figures of contemporary dance.

"But," Merce said, smiling, "as one perceptive out-of-town critic wrote, 'It's not that Cunningham's gone establishment, but that the Establishment has gone Cunningham.'"

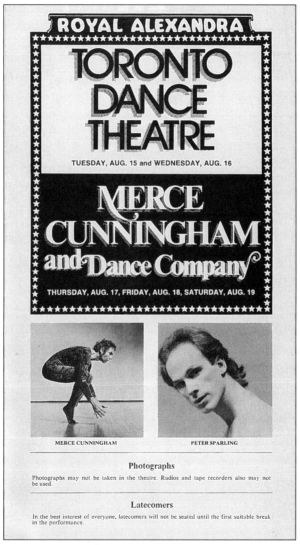

*Playbill for the Merce Cunningham
Dance Company, 1978.*

Still, as late as 1974, when the Boston Ballet presented two Cunningham works, audiences loved the lyric *Summerspace*, but stormed out of the controversial *Winterbranch* in waves. Yet, as Merce explained, "There's no great mystery surrounding the dances. The spectator has to be willing to forget preconceived notions of what dance should be—that it should tell a story or illustrate a piece of music—and simply look at what is going on.

"There's the shifting relationships between dancers, the way space constantly changes, the sculptural groupings that appear and dissolve, the passages of fast footwork."

I watched one of the dance group's rehearsals one day with fascination. Merce sat on a chair at the edge of the stage, watching intently as his dancers went through a complex series of configurations, checking their timing with a stopwatch. The rehearsal was conducted in a silence broken only by the dancers' breathing, the sound of their feet marking the rhythm, and the odd gasp of laughter when someone missed a catch.

Between sequences, the dancers practised singly or in pairs, flopped to the floor, or chatted quietly in groups, while Merce jotted notes on a pad. At times he'd walk around, talking quietly to one or two dancers, demonstrating technical points with swift, graphic gestures.

Then, returning to his seat, he'd say softly, "All right, let's do it again," and the dancing resumed.

"You have to love dancing to stick to it," he said. "It gives you nothing back, no manuscripts to store away, no paintings to hang on walls or show in museums, no poems to be printed and sold, nothing but that single fleeting moment when you feel alive."

One of my favourite nights in our new Princess of Wales theatre was March 4, 1996. It was a special event called "The Ed Mirvish Tribute," sponsored by the Toronto Entertainment District Association.

Let me briefly pause to explain what that is. Toronto's entertainment district is first of all a neighbourhood—a safe and vibrant section of the downtown core embracing numerous world-class attractions. Within its boundaries are such famous structures as the SkyDome, home of the Blue Jays; the geodesic-domed Ontario Place on the lakefront with its Molson Amphitheatre; the CN Tower, tallest in the world at 1,815 feet; Harbourfront, internationally renowned for its literary readings; the Metro Convention Centre; Roy Thomson

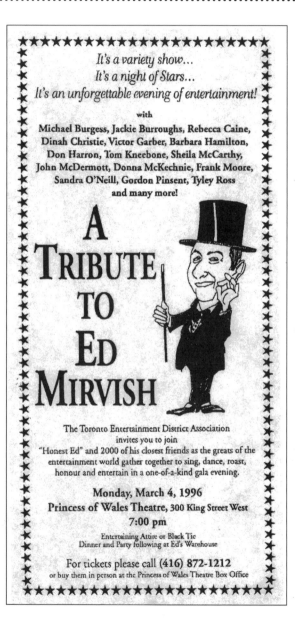

Concert Hall (with 2,800 seats); Hummingbird Centre theatre (3,200 seats); the Royal Alexandra theatre (1,500 seats); and the Princess of Wales theatre (2,000 seats).

The area is also filled with scores of excellent restaurants and quality hotels, while thousands of artisans ply and display their crafts within the area's boundaries.

The job of the Toronto Entertainment District Association is to support, develop, and promote the neighbourhood as North America's most diverse entertainment area. And, on the night of my tribute, the association said, "Ed Mirvish's considerable contributions have strengthened and expanded the district immeasurably."

It was a night of magic and boundless talent. Co-chaired by Bill Ballard and Peter Soumalias, no budget could cover the cost of the producers, directors, designers, choreographers, stagehands, musicians, and massive cast that these men assembled. Rarely, if ever, has a cast of this size and calibre been assembled on one stage for a single evening's performance.

Except for a special nod to Hal Linden and Donald O'Connor who flew in from the States, the number of

Only a few of my closest 2,000 friends are listed in this advertisement inviting people to attend the tribute for me held by the Toronto Entertainment District Association.

individual stars who appeared is too long to list, but I thank them all from my heart.

It was Bill Ballard's idea to introduce another group of people who had never appeared on stage—a cross-section of our various employees who've worked with me over the years. They were called from the sidelines and individually introduced by name, position, and length of service. And these, I will name out of gratitude:

> Tony Falico, Ed's former parking lot attendant; head chef of Ed's Restaurant, 40 years
> Russell Lazar, general manager and buyer at Honest Ed's, 39 years
> Mary Liska, accounts payable, Honest Ed's, 39 years
> Lou Peck, buyer, Honest Ed's, 39 years
> Willie Mihalik, maitre'd, Ed's Warehouse, 31 years
> Barbara Jupzinski, cleaning department supervisor for the theatres and restaurants, 31 years
> Phillip Lew, waiter, Ed's Warehouse, 26 years
> Mavis Smarthe, security, Honest Ed's, 25 years

This is our part of the neighbourhood, which includes other tourist attractions within a few short blocks—Roy Thomson Hall, SkyDome, the CN Tower, and more. It's a colourful and lively area. I try to get down here every day.

Robert Sheridan, assistant buyer, Honest Ed's, 23 years

Llowellyn Mullings, assistant buyer, Honest Ed's, 22 years

Yale Simpson, childhood friend, general manager of Royal Alex for 25 years; general manager of Ed's Restaurants for past 33 years; business associate over 65 years

To me, they're *all* stars.

In 1978, the Alex staged that bloodthirsty Broadway hit, *Dracula*. It starred Jean Leclerc, the 32-year-old Montreal actor who, during Frank Langella's absence from the long-running New York production, had played the notorious Count to sensational reviews.

Many critics also hailed Jean as "the new Louis Jourdan." When I asked how he felt about it, he simply shrugged and said if Americans saw him that way, he wasn't about to object. No such comparison had ever

The cover of our magazine to celebrate 90 years of theatre at the Royal Alex.

been made in Quebec where, for the previous 12 years, he'd established a solid identity all his own on stage, in films, and on TV. Nor at Stratford, where he played in three productions.

"But in New York," as Jean pointed out, "no matter how much previous work you've done, nor how much experience you've acquired, they like to think they've discovered you."

Leclerc was actually "discovered" by New Yorkers in the CBC's production of "Sarah," which aired earlier that year on PBS, in which he played Jacques Damala, actress Sarah Bernhardt's drug-addicted young husband. A month later he got a message through his Montreal answering service asking him to call the Jeffery Johnson Casting Agency in New York.

When he called, the agency said it was interested in him for *Dracula*. "It's since become a standing joke there," Jean said, grinning, "that the first thing I asked was what part they had in mind. I had no idea they were considering me for the lead."

In New York two days later, he was given the script and was told to meet the producers at the Martin Beck theatre at ten the next morning. When he arrived, all the doors were locked. "I thought how strange that they'd ask me to meet them and then not show up."

Someone finally told him the box office didn't open

till eleven and suggested he try the stage door. "It hadn't even occurred to me," he said. "So much for my savoir faire." The stage doorman asked Jean where he'd been, then directed him down a corridor which led to the stage.

"I wandered on out into the glare of the rehearsal light carrying my raincoat, and a voice called out from the black depths of the theatre, 'Okay, we're ready for the first scene.'

"It was hardly what I'd expected. I thought I'd just meet the producers and talk about the play. But then, someone was throwing me a cue line, so I started reading the script, completely unprepared.

"Then a man jumped on stage and said, 'Fine. Now do it again at the top of your voice. I want to find out if you can fill the theatre.' It was the director, Dennis Rosa. I did the scene again, projecting as loudly as I could, until Rosa stopped me and said, 'Thank you very much for coming.'"

Jean was heading out, convinced he'd blown it, when an assistant director stopped him and said, "Go have a coffee, and come back in an hour." So he waited in the stage door entrance and asked the doorman if any other actors had auditioned that morning. "A few," the man replied, and Jean's heart sank. Then the doorman said, "That's a good voice you got there. Heard you all the way back here. Didn't hear the others, but I heard you." And Jean's hopes rose.

"Finally," he said, "I started laughing, when I realized what I must have looked like. Naïve kid from the sticks walking on stage with a gee-whiz look. So I decided not to make any more of an ass of myself than I already had. When I was called back to repeat my lines, I felt I had nothing to lose so I had no nerves at all. There was dead silence out front when I finished. So I casually said, 'I expect my French accent is too strong,' and someone shouted out, 'No, we love it.'"

He was told to report to the Johnson agency at three. Jean went to his hotel, took a shower, changed clothes— then went out and walked around in the rain. "I don't remember where I went, or what I did. I'm surprised I wasn't run over crossing streets."

At the agency, Jeffery Johnson asked him how the audition had gone. Jean told him, "Very badly. I was nervous, excited, and hadn't expected to be asked to read. Then I read too fast, and tripped over my accent." Johnson interrupted to say that the producers had been tremendously impressed, and Jean would hear from them.

"I was stunned," Jean said. "I felt like I'd been hit by a rock. That evening I had dinner with Dennis Rosa. I thought we'd discuss the production, but we talked about everything else instead.

"The only thing Dennis said about *Dracula* was, 'Just make sure you get the business with the cape right. It weighs twenty-five pounds, and it's hard to twirl.'"

And that, said Jean, is how he got the role.

In 1988, David and I were delighted to announce the appointment of Jonathan Miller as artistic director of the Old Vic.

Before the brilliant Dr. Miller took over, he gave us about 25 scripts of potential plays to pore over. I looked at the first few and was totally flummoxed. Finally, I asked Jonathan what they were. "Well, actually, Ed," he said with a smile, "most of them are eighteenth-century translations."

Thank God for David. He was actually fascinated by them. So I left him and Jonathan to make the decisions. I'd never have been able to plough through that pile.

But by the end of Jonathan's three-year directorship, I must say this. The Old Vic had won more Olivier Awards than either the Royal Shakespeare Theatre or the National Theatre. I also seriously suspect that the work Jonathan did had a certain effect on my being named a Commander of the British Empire at the time.

Programs from some of the plays for which Jonathan Miller was artistic director.

*A proud day at Buckingham Palace. I think I have the
talents of Jonathan Miller partially to thank for my being
named a Commander of the British Empire, for he brought
great glory to the Old Vic.*

I went to Buckingham Palace and was so honoured by the Queen.

Jonathan's tenure was a period of prestige and countless accolades. But we didn't exactly break box office records. Whenever I saw Dr. Miller, I'd say, "If you ever get the urge to make money, Jonathan, don't fight it."

I n years past, the Old Vic Theatre had distinguished repertory companies under the guidance of Sir Tyrone Guthrie and Sir Laurence Olivier.

In March 1997, we introduced a third rep company at the Old Vic under a third knight—Sir Peter Hall.

One of the great names of British theatre, Sir Peter founded the Royal Shakespeare Company and was formerly artistic director of both the Royal National Theatre and the Glyndebourne Festival. Now as the Old Vic's artistic director, he heads the Peter Hall Company.

Still amazingly energetic at 65, he's known as a strict disciplinarian. His usual routine is to rise at six, drink a pot of tea, give two hours' dictation, do exercises and make telephone calls, all before his taxi picks him up at nine to take him to the theatre. Planning, strategy, and

*Sir Peter Hall is announced as artistic director
of the Old Vic.*

Sir Peter Hall is announced as artistic director of the Old Vic.

A little bit of Canada visits my little bit of England. This gang is the Board of Governors of the National Theatre School of Canada on a trip to the Old Vic in 1989. Our son David is at the extreme right.

only governments and charitable organizations can usually afford to subsidize. But still, I said, we'll never know unless we try it. Let's do it for a year and see if we can afford it.

Both the Royal Shakespeare Company and the Royal National Theatre run rep companies of their own, but there's a refreshing difference to Hall's idea that might breathe new life and deliver new talent into British theatre.

Each season will consist of twelve plays, six classic and six contemporary. In 1997, the dramas included Shakespeare's *King Lear*, Chekhov's *The Seagull* (in a new translation by Tom Stoppard), Beckett's *Waiting for Godot* (the play that made Hall famous when he directed its English-language world première in 1955), Harley Granville-Barker's *Waste* (banned for three decades after its 1907 debut), and David Rabe's *Hurlyburly*.

While the classics are indeed drawing audiences, it's the new plays by unknown writers we hope will make the biggest impact. As Sir Peter says, "The great thing for the authors is that they will have fully rehearsed, fully cast productions in a major theatre, reviewed by critics. And because we intend to run those shows for only six performances and one preview initially, they won't be facing the humiliation, and cost, of a failed run.

Michael Pennington in Waste, *directed by Sir Peter Hall in March 1997.*

"If the piece *does* work, it can move into the repertory and continue to be played. At the end of the season, if it's successful, it can also move to a West End theatre, or be sent on the road. So it's basically a three-tiered plan. The West End doesn't do new plays anymore—the risk is too great—so there's a huge need for a new play space that's fairly big and accommodating."

Both Sir Peter and David agreed to concentrate on playwrights from the eighties and nineties because, as Hall points out, "the more established writers are all quite properly ensconced at the National or Royal Shakespeare. But there's a generation of actors and playwrights who are working on the fringe, waiting to get in the queue for the major stages. Meantime, a lot get snapped up by television, and you never see them again."

From his 40 years of experience, Hall has picked a core of 25 superb actors. They include such stars as Oscar-winner Ben Kingsley (in *Godot*), American actress Elizabeth McGovern, Rupert Graves (from *Trainspotting*) and Victora Hamilton, who starred at the Royal Alex with Alan Bates in *The Master Builder*.

The actors perform in different shows seven days a week for 40 weeks—the first time a major London theatre has been open every day of the week. Which means that even overseas visitors might be able to catch six different plays, three classic and three contemporary, in a single week.

But don't expect shows with mega-musical values. All productions have a "single-unit set," a basic design

that stays put for each play, while the lighting, furniture, props, and costumes rotate. Sir Peter says, "We spend far too much money in rep companies these days changing sets for each show. A single-unit set allows the actors to act immediately on stage, since we won't have to clear out while a new set gets built."

Both David and I realize that rotating shows offer a higher risk than mounting a commercial run of a single production. But we've cut ticket prices across the board, making us more financially accessible than West End theatres. And we're also offering memberships that give further discounts and first-choice seating to the shorter runs of the new plays.

Then too, as David says, it's attractive to the performers, because the actor playing Lear, for instance, won't be stuck doing the shows eight times a week. That's just too often to get consistently strong work. They do it twice a week instead, leaving them free to do other things, like film, and leaving us time to build an audience between performances.

When the season opened, the reviews for all plays were generally ecstatic. Yet the show that hit the head-

Appearing in The Master Builder *with Alan Bates was Victoria Hamilton, one of the actors hand-picked by Peter Hall to be part of a new rep company.*

lines was the première of *Hurlyburly*, Rabe's disturbing portrait of cocaine-snorting Hollywood buddies with their macho male bonding and easy women.

Just 15 minutes before the final curtain, Rupert Graves was on stage reading a letter from a friend that stated that "death is the essence of destiny." Just then, the stage manager walked out and said, "Ladies and gentlemen, I'm sorry to interrupt, but due to unforeseen circumstances, would you all kindly stand up and leave the building in an orderly fashion."

No one in the audience knew, of course, that the "unforeseen circumstances" was actually a bomb threat delivered to the stage door. But everyone filed out in proper English order. And once outside, it was announced with theatrical flair that the show would go on.

With which Graves, Elizabeth McGovern, and company mounted benches encircling a tree in a small seedy park across the street and took the play to its conclusion.

It naturally got a standing ovation, since the audience was already standing. But the applause was long and boisterous. Even passers-by on the street joined in.

Nevertheless, we could do without any more bomb scares. Yet we sincerely hope the applause will continue for Sir Peter Hall's superb new company. As the London *Daily Telegraph's* critic wrote, "It's a joyous display of young star talent."

Until she died in her eighty-third year, my mother used to say, "Ed, you have two main faults. One, you're never satisfied. Two, you talk too much."

I only wish she'd been there the day I was sitting in my office at the Royal Alexandra when Peter O'Toole walked in. Peter started talking the second he sat down. He was starring in *Uncle Vanya* at the time and wanted to tell me about some great bar he'd discovered where he'd just drunk lunch.

Then, in the middle of his oration, in walked the Canadian playwright Bernie Slade, followed by the eminent producer Morton Gottlieb, who'd produced Bernie's *Same Time, Next Year* on Broadway. We were planning to stage the show, and the two had come by to discuss it. But Peter was building to a climax, so they patiently heard him out.

Then, just as Gottlieb started to speak, the door popped open again, and in walked Jack Lemmon, who was in town promoting a movie. There were handshakes and backslaps all around, and all four of them started talking at once. It was like an instant cocktail party and went

on for nearly two hours. The guys had an obvious ball.

But the point of the story is this. My mother, bless her, would have been proud of me. For during the entire gabfest, I simply sat and listened. In fact, I couldn't get a word in edgewise.

Put two stars, a producer, and playwright in a room and they'll put on a whole show by themselves.

I f Neil Simon has been the Royal Alex's most prolific supplier of comedies, George Gershwin gave it the most musicals during his short life—and even long after his death.

Porgy and Bess, the most popular opera ever written by an American, has played the Alex numerous times through the years since it first played here in the 1930s. And as recently as 1996, we ran the hugely popular

We finally did put on Same Time, Next Year. *It was hard to talk business with such entertaining story tellers as Peter O'Toole and Jack Lemmon arriving all at once. Discussions with Bernie Slade and his producer were put on the back burner for a few hours while, for once, I sat and listened.*

*Actor Jim Walton surrounded by some of the chorus girls
from* Crazy for You.

Crazy for You, featuring Gershwin's songs (and the
immortal Mickey Rooney).

Following Gershwin's first big Broadway success,
Lady Be Good, in 1924, the Alex staged the road shows
of his new musicals almost yearly for a decade—such
hits as *Tip-Toes, Oh, Kay!, Funny Face, Girl Crazy, Strike
Up the Band*, and *Of Thee I Sing*.

And, judging from the theatre's old ledgers, the
shows were all hits. But, then again, so was Gershwin at
the time. With his sleek good looks, endless energy and
charm, joy in his own talent, and charisma surpassing

most film stars, George was not only a 1920s Renaissance man, but America's first superstar of Scott Fitzgerald's "Jazz Age."

Besides composing, he was a virtuoso pianist, regularly playing his own music with symphony orchestras, and often conducting his own works, as well. He frequently appeared five times a day at the leading movie palaces and had his own weekly radio show. To "relax" at night, he'd play piano for two or three hours at the best party in town, surrounded by famous faces.

Born in 1898 to Russian immigrants, George grew up to the rhythms of a new century. When jazz floated up from New Orleans to Chicago then headed east into Harlem, George and his brother Ira haunted the new jazz clubs before they were into long pants.

When their mother, Rose, bought a second-hand piano for Ira, it was George who took over the keyboard, playing the day's hit melodies by ear. So it was George who was sent off for 50-cent piano lessons, while Ira stayed home and read.

While Ira stayed in high school, editing its newspaper, George quit at 15 to become "the youngest piano pounder ever employed in Tin Pan Alley" at $15 a week, and soon added to his income by making piano rolls on weekends. But when he offered one of his own compositions to his

*Here are Mickey Rooney and Barbara Hamilton in their
roles in* Crazy for You *(top left and above)...and here we
are just having fun (left).*

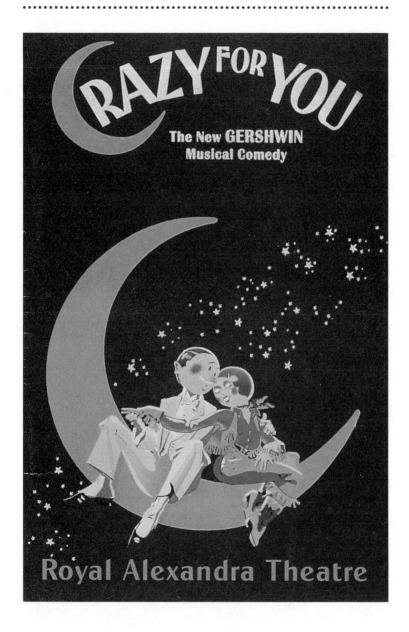

employers, he was told, "You're here as a pianist, not a composer."

When he finally sold his first tune, "When You Want 'Em, You Can't Get 'Em," he got five bucks. And for his first Broadway composition, "Making of a Girl" in a 1916 Shubert production, he got $7. But it encouraged him to quit his job as a song plugger and turn to "production music." Meanwhile Ira was looking for a composer for his lyrics, and in 1918 they had the first of their famous Broadway collaborations with *The Real American Folk Song*.

Throughout the Roaring Twenties, the hit tunes rolled out: "Rhapsody in Blue," "Lady Be Good," "Fascinating Rhythm," "Someone to Watch Over Me," "S'Wonderful," "I've Got Rhythm," "American in Paris." So did the shows. George was America's darling. Yet when *Of Thee I Sing* became the first musical to win a Pulitzer Prize, the award went to Ira for his lyrics. George wasn't mentioned.

The composer took it in stride. After all, he'd once written a song in less than an hour for the Broadway smash *La, La Lucille*. The tune won no acclaim—until Al Jolson heard Gershwin sing it at a party one night and

"Crazy for You" sums up how I feel about my foray into the theatre world. I wouldn't have missed it for anything.

decided to add it to his hit musical *Sinbad*. Of course, it became part of musical history the moment Al Jolson sang "Swanee."

The brothers shared a major disappointment when the masterpiece *Porgy and Bess* opened in 1935 to mixed reviews. It wasn't considered an American classic until its revivals following George's death two years later. He and Ira were working on *The Goldwyn Follies* when George began getting excruciating headaches. On a rainy Sunday morning in 1937, America's brilliant Renaissance Man died. He was 38.

But his music has lived on, and always will. Over the decades it has thrilled the crowds at the Royal Alexandra, as it has the rest of the world.

J olson: *The Musical* opened to packed houses and rave reviews at the Royal Alex in June 1997. Starring the sensational Brian Conley, it came directly from London's West End, where it had won the Olivier Award for best musical the year before.

The show, packed with such famous Al Jolson hits as "Swanee," "Baby Face," "Sonny Boy," and "My Mammy," traces the singer's life from the time he fled his

Full circle: Jolson himself performed at the Royal Alex. Now we have Brian Conley, above, starring in Jolson: The Musical.

Lithuanian rabbi father's home in 1897 at age eleven to join Rich and Hoppe's Big Company of Fun Makers, to his death in 1950 while entertaining American troops in Korea.

It was fitting indeed that our storied old King Street theatre would present the musical's North American première, for Jolson himself had played the Alex in eight separate shows between 1913 and 1941—the years encompassing his heyday as "The World's Greatest Entertainer," a sobriquet Al not only admitted to but probably instigated.

His 1913 appearance was in *The Whirl of Society*, co-starring Fanny Brice, followed two years later by *Dancing Around*, which featured the star in his signature blackface. Hailed as a "torrid tempest of terpsichorean triumphs," it promised Jolson with "dozens of dainty dimpled divinities." (And they used to call my own ad promotions florid.)

When Al returned in 1920 with *Sinbad*, the show that finally made Gershwin's "Swanee" famous, Jolson was deified by one inanely alliterative Toronto critic as "the Vesuvius of vocal velocity and chief cook of jocular joys." Regardless of how it must have stroked Al's already Hindenberg-sized ego, one can only hope the critic was thereafter relegated to writing obits.

Fortunately, by the time of Jolson's final Royal Alex

appearance in 1941's *Hold On to Your Hats*, a more distinguished critic sat among the wartime audience. Prior to becoming one of Canada's greatest novelists, Robertson Davies (as literary editor of *Saturday Night*) had misgivings about the show—such as the dog that snarled each time Hitler's name was mentioned—but was fulsome in his praise of the star.

"Al Jolson has personality and technique of a very rare order," Davies wrote. "He has a phenomenal ability to make himself likeable, whatever he does.

"Personally I cannot abide his sentimental songs or his quasi-pathetic Yiddish humour, but I have the highest regard for the man himself: my attitude toward him is that of a Pilgrim Father toward a charming tavern-keeper, for I love the sinner while hating his sin.

"But Al Jolson has a winning way and a surety of touch, a rapport with the audience which would spread a guffaw through the pews of a tabernacle. Such ability commands respect and there is no doubt that, within the limits of his personality (which is very extensive) and his material (which is very narrow), he is an artist of the highest order, and one whom no student of the theatre should neglect [to] see and study."

Yet, unrelated to Jolson, Davies had one major gripe that, considering the pulsing, ear-shattering over-amplification of today's rock extravaganzas, seems prophetic. "On the debit side," he gnashed, "the microphones must come first. Are modern singers so lacking in volume that they cannot make themselves heard without these abominations? A pox on all public-address systems."

Since then, both Al Jolson and Robertson Davies have left the orb of a live stage's spotlight. Only the microphones remain.

But the memory of each amazing artist remains with us: Davies through his words, Jolson through his songs.

Yet, ironically, the young Canadian critic's name is today more universally renowned for his contribution to the arts than the world's greatest entertainer he so glowingly wrote about.

Epilogue

I've had a wonderful life. It's allowed me to be a store-keeper for 68 years, a theatre owner for 34, and a restaurateur for 31—and run all three businesses simultaneously.

And the best thing about them all is meeting hundreds of people every day from all walks of life.

I meet the customers in Honest Ed's discount store each morning and afternoon, and in Old Ed's restaurant each day at lunch. In these separate establishments, I've made a lot of friends. It's always a delight when they tell me they've just had a great bargain or a fine meal.

But the biggest thrill of all, of course, is meeting the thousands of patrons who pour into our three theatres each night. When you see them roar to their feet at the end of a play, then leave the theatre glowing with the enjoyment of the night, there's nothing else quite like it in the world.

For unlike the selling of merchandise or food, what you're putting on display is a stage full of people. Patrons purchase tickets not to buy a lawnmower or a roast beef dinner, but to see great stars entertain them.

No lawnmower or meal ever aroused an entire room to silent tears or gales of laughter.

What we sell in a theatre are a writer's ideas, an actor's stagecraft, a composer's music, a choreographer's flowing dances—an escape from the real world. Theatre is entirely a people business.

And that includes the artists both behind the stage and on it. I am constantly amazed at the sudden sight of a teeming Saigon street, which you know is built with plywood. And I'm forever awed at a fellow human who can bring *King Lear* to life before your eyes.

Ah, those wonderful actors (with few exceptions) I've met and come to know through the decades. Their presence, their stories, their sense of joy—which I've tried to relate in these pages. I've loved the hours with them.

It was one of those actors who gave me the best piece of advice I've had. Ever since reaching my seventies, I've had a snap comeback when someone wants me to commit to something in the future. "Listen," I say, "at *my* age I don't even buy green bananas."

On my last meeting with Hume Cronyn, he heard me spout that line. "Don't *ever* say that, Ed," he said softly. "Keep on buying green bananas."

He made me think, and be thankful. And I haven't said it since.

Now at 83, I look forward to seeing those green bananas ripen.

Index

Photo Credits

Page 2: Boris Spremo, Toronto Star; 18: Metropolitan Toronto Reference Library, T 18086; 27: Courtesy of the Governors of the Old Vic; 28: Enthoven Collection, Victoria and Albert Museum; 42: Ken Kerr, Toronto Sun; 50: John McNeill, Globe and Mail; 97: Michael Cooper Photographic; 112: Sir George; 114: R. Lazar; 126: Tom Sandler Photography; 140: Jay Thompson, L.A.; 155: Nir Bareket Photography; 156: Nir Bareket Photography; 166: BBC Pictorial Publicity; 204: Gary Wilson; 206: Walter Paré; 208: John Haynes; 216: Michael Cooper; 219: Michael Cooper.